To Bud on Christmas 1949
From Janet, Joe & Norb

John Bran[...]
2730 Posh Rd
Des Moines, Ia

THE CREED IN SLOW MOTION

THE CREED
IN SLOW MOTION

By
RONALD KNOX

NEW YORK
SHEED & WARD
1949

Nihil obstat: Reginaldus Phillips, S.T.L.
                        Censor deputatus
Imprimatur: E. Morrogh Bernard
                        Vic. Gen.
Westmonasterii, die 8a Novembris, 1948

. . . AND CLAUDIA

AUTHOR'S NOTE

THE SERMONS of which this book is composed were delivered to the girls at the Assumption Convent (now at Exton, Rutland) when they were evacuated to Aldenham Park, Bridgnorth, during the late war.

CONTENTS

I

I believe in God (1)

MORE AND more, the longer I stay here, and the
longer some of you stay here, do I find it difficult
to preach to you. At Oxford, where the ordinary
undergraduate only lasted three years, it was quite
simple, because at the end of three years I started
preaching the same sermons over again. But here
it's different. If you come to think of it—it's a dreadful thing to reflect about—we have been three years
here together; and when I look round I still see a lot
of the same old faces, that is, rather older faces, but
still recognizably the same. And whereas I know you
remember very little of what I say to you in sermons,
I am quite confident you would spot it if I started
preaching the same sermons over again; none of you
would have any idea what I was going to say next,
but there would be a general groan of " We've had
that one before ". So, as it's difficult to go on from
one Sunday to the next thinking up a new subject
to preach about, I am going to start this year by
launching out on a course, and a course which will see
us through more than a month of Sundays. I'm going
to give you an exposition, clause by clause, of the
Apostles' Creed; that is, the *Credo* which we learn in
our Catechism, not the longer and more difficult
one which is said at Mass. That will mean, I am afraid,
something more like an instruction than a sermon

properly so called. And you will be inclined to complain, perhaps, that it is too much like lessons, and you get quite enough lessons as it is in the course of the week. But I thought if we managed to make these instructions fairly chatty and informal, it won't matter so much.

Well, we are starting off this afternoon with " I believe in God "; that ought to last us for the length of a whole sermon, even if we cut it down as much as we can. Let me direct your attention first of all to the use of the word " I ". Surely that's curious, if you come to think of it? Surely saying the *Credo* ought to be a tremendous congregational act, uniting us in a common profession of faith, and surely at that rate it ought to start " WE believe "? But it doesn't, you see, ever take that form. Go out to Lourdes, and watch from the top of the slope tens of thousands of candles flickering there below, in the torch-light procession. So many of them, they don't look like separate candles; it is just a vast haze of light. And the people who carry them are singing *Credo; Credo*, not *Credimus*. And so it is at Mass. If you watch the *Gloria*, it is *we* all through, *Laudamus te, Benedicimus te, Adoramus te, Glorificamus te*, and so on; we lose ourselves in a crowd when we are singing the *Gloria*. But when we sing the *Credo*, we are not meant to lose ourselves in a crowd. Every clause of it is the expression of my opinion, for which I am personally responsible. Just so with the *Confiteor*; it is always *Confiteor* we say, not *Confitemur*, even when we are saying it together. Why? Because my sins are my sins, and your sins are your sins; each of us is individually responsible. So it is with the *Credo*; each of us, in lonely isolation, makes himself or herself responsible for that tremendous statement, " I believe in God ".

I expect you will think I have been making too much of that, and rather wasting time over a minor point. Believe me, it isn't so. The reason why I want to give you this course of sermons on the *Credo* is because I want each of you to say it intelligently, thinking what you are saying, meaning what you are saying, not just copying the girl next you, not just reciting a rigmarole of words which must be all right, of course, or the Church wouldn't make you say it. No, you are to say the *Credo* as an expression of your own individual point of view, giving it the full homage of your intellect, prepared to explain it to other people; if necessary, to argue it with other people. I, Mary Smith, believe in God.

" I believe "—we have often been told that we ought to be proud of our faith. But there's a tendency and a temptation for us, on the contrary, to be ashamed of our faith when we are living among people who don't agree with us; we don't like the idea of believing so much more than they do. Because, after all, the person who is ready to believe anything you tell her —on the first of April, for example—is a person who doesn't command your respect. I don't say we should go so far as to call such a person a mug, because that wouldn't be a ladylike word to use, but we think of her as a mug. Credulity—by which I mean the quality of being a mug—is a weakness in a human character; and at the back of our minds, I think, we have always got the idea that the less you believe the more clever and the more enlightened you must be.

Well, of course that comes from looking at the thing in quite the wrong way. The difference between being a credulous person (or mug) and being a sensible person isn't a question of HOW MANY things you believe; it's a question of whether you believe the RIGHT things; that is to say, whether you demand the right kind of evidence before you believe a thing or not. I mean, if you take a perfectly open question like the Loch Ness Monster: it's foolish to believe a story of that kind merely because you've seen an article in a picture paper about it, which would notoriously say anything. On the other hand, if you've been about in that part of the world and met various people whom you regard as sensible, truthful people, who say they've seen the thing, then it is foolish NOT to believe in it.

No, don't let's be got down just because we come across other people who haven't as much belief as we have. Very likely they haven't come across the evidences for the Christian religion as we have. Or perhaps they have come across them and not been able to estimate them at their true worth; in that case, it is they who are the mugs, not we. Of all the silly things on which the modern world prides itself, the silliest, I think, is its habit of not believing in things. Nothing is easier than not believing in things.

Anyhow, you believe. You believe, because you regard the Catholic Church as a trustworthy source of information. We shall get on to that subject, towards the end of the *Credo*, if we live long enough, so we won't stop over it here. But it's worth while observing that not all the articles in the *Credo* have to be believed on the authority of the Church. The very

subject we are discussing this afternoon (if we find
we have time enough to discuss it), the existence of
God, isn't a belief that depends merely on the authority of the Church. The existence of God can be proved
by the use of reason.

And again, the statement that Jesus Christ was
crucified under Pontius Pilate isn't a belief which
depends on the authority of the Church. All sorts of
authorities, Josephus for example, who wasn't a
Christian but a Jew, assure us that a man called
Pontius Pilate was procurator of Judaea under the
emperor Tiberius. And there's nothing at all improbable about a particular Galilean being crucified
about that time. Some thirty years before, 2,000
Galileans were crucified by the orders of the Roman
governor by one edict. It's simply a matter of history,
and there is no reason to doubt it.

" But," you say, " if these things are quite obviously
true, as a matter of philosophy or as a matter of history,
why should I have to get up and assert my belief that
they are true? Surely everybody, Christian or not,
must believe in them." Well, that's the curious thing,
there are quite a lot of perfectly intelligent people
going about who don't really *believe* in these things.
If you ask them whether they believe God exists,
they will say, " Oh, yes, I suppose so ". If you ask
them whether Jesus Christ was crucified under
Pontius Pilate, they will say, " Yes, the evidence for
that seems quite conclusive ". But there the thing
stops, they don't do anything about it. They are
unable to deny these truths, but these truths don't
form part of the framework of their minds. To *believe*
a thing, in any sense worth the name, means something

much more than merely not denying it. It means focusing your mind on it, letting it haunt your imagination, caring, and caring desperately, whether it is true or not. Put it in this way. If somebody says to you, " Of course, your own country's rule in the Colonies is every bit as brutal as German rule in Poland ", you don't reply, " Oh, really? I dare say it is ". You care furiously about a statement like that. You may not have the facts at your fingers' ends, but you are not going to let a statement like that pass without examination. It would alter your whole idea of what the world is like if you thought a statement like that could be true. And it has, or it ought to have, the same sort of effect, if somebody tells you that some article of the Christian creed isn't true. The same sort of effect, only much worse. Because if you thought *that*, it wouldn't merely alter your whole idea of what the world was like; it would alter your whole idea about this world and the next, about what life means and why we human beings have been put into the world at all. If you really *believe* a thing, it becomes part of the make-up of your mind; it lends coherence to your thought, colour to your imagination, leverage to your will. It *matters* enormously; to lose your belief would dislocate your whole life. That is what we mean, among other things, when we say the *Credo*.

But at the same time, we mustn't imagine, we mustn't for a moment imagine, that we haven't got to *think* about our faith, that we have done our duty as Catholics if we simply shout about the faith, instead of thinking about it. That is a notion which is widely current outside the Church, and I'm sorry to say that I think we Catholics are partly to blame for giving that impression. I mean, you will come across non-Catholics who will say, " How nice it must be to be a Catholic, and not have to think about one's religion! To have the whole thing done for one, just be told by the Church what one is to believe and what one isn't to believe, and no more worry about it! " The odd thing is that people who talk like that are really quite sincere about it; they do genuinely think that is the Catholic attitude, and in a way they rather envy us. Everybody likes avoiding a job of work, and especially a job of intellectual work. And, you know, I think there is a temptation for us Catholics to play up to that lead, and to sham stupid, as it were, when we find ourselves in the middle of a religious discussion. You might find yourself, for example, among a set of people who were discussing whether the soul is or is not immortal, whether there is or is not a life beyond the grave. And your simplest plan, if somebody turns to you and asks what you think about it, is to say, " Well, you see, I'm a Catholic, and the Catholic Church teaches me that there is a future life, so of course I've got to believe it ". And that's true; but it's not the whole truth. There are perfectly good grounds on which you can tackle a person who says the soul is destroyed at death; not perhaps so as to convince him of the contrary, but at least to show him that he can't prove his case. And those grounds you, as a Catholic, ought to know; not for your own sake so much as for the sake of other people. You want to be able to help them in their difficulties, not just sit by with a superior air and congratulate yourself on being better off than they are, as if you were a person who had saved up your sweet ration and they hadn't saved up theirs.

I know you think all this sounds very remote and improbable, but it won't seem like that in a few years' time. It may easily happen, for example, that you'll fall in love with somebody who isn't a Catholic and want to marry him. I very much hope that that won't happen; if only because I know from experience that there are a lot of Catholic young men going about who are badly in need of marrying Catholic wives. But on the law of averages the thing is pretty likely to happen, and if it does, you will want the young man to get converted. And he will want to get converted, because he will think you are rather a nice kind of person, and it must have been a rather nice religion that produced a person like that. Now, if he gets the impression that your faith is merely a matter of shutting your eyes and believing things are true just because you want them to be true, it will have a bad effect on him. Either it will put him off the Church, because that way of going about it doesn't seem to him to be honest. Or he will go and get instructed by a priest, and say " Splendid! That's absolutely all right by me " to everything the priest tells him, without really finding out what it's all about and digesting what he's told; and that means another half-baked convert. Whereas, if he gets the idea that you mean what you say when you say (for example) " I believe in God ", that you have really formed your mind on the subject and faced the difficulties and made the doctrine your own, then he will have more respect for your religion and, in the long run, more respect for you.

There, I knew what would happen. We haven't

left time to talk about the subject I meant to talk about this afternoon, which was, if you remember, that of belief in God. But, all the same, I don't think we shall have been wasting our time if I've got you to see that believing a thing doesn't merely mean admitting its truth because you can't see your way to denying it. Believing a thing (in the theological sense) means embracing it as something you are going to live by. And on the other hand, believing a thing does mean knowing what you are talking about, using your brains over it, not merely shouting it out as a slogan. Belief isn't just a matter of the intellect, isn't just a matter of the will; it is an activity of the whole man.

II

I believe in God (2)

WHEN ADAM and Eve first sinned, in Paradise, it was their instinct to avoid the presence of their Creator. It's not easy, and I don't think it's very important, to decide how much the details in that story are to be taken quite literally, and how much we may think of them as a poetic description of what happened. But what we are told is that they heard the voice of the Lord God walking in the garden in the afternoon air, and they were afraid; so they hid themselves among the trees of the garden. If we find it difficult to be certain how literally we ought to take the details of the story, we are not tempted to doubt, for a moment, that the story is true. For this story of the Fall is a story we live through, most of us, not once but many times in the course of our lives. It is a drama in which we ourselves are the actors, and the story repeats itself. When we have sinned, the thought of God makes us feel uncomfortable, and we try to forget it. And the human race, which is always sinning, is always trying to forget God. Man tries to shut himself up, hide himself away, in this forest of created things which God has given us for our enjoyment; he tries to pretend to himself that God doesn't exist. But, as he looks out through the long avenues of the tree trunks, first down one, then down another, he sees at the end of each vista the same sight; it is the face of God. He cannot get away from God even when he wants to.

What do I mean? Why, this; that even if no revelation had come to us through Jesus Christ, we should still have to admit, if we would be honest with ourselves, the existence of God—however unwelcome that thought might be. The creatures that surround us, and our own life in this world of creatures, lead us to the acknowledgement that God exists. If we take any of our favourite trains of thought, and follow it out far enough, it spreads away into the distance like some forest ride, and we see, very far off, God at the end of it.

It's an inveterate habit of man to ask "Why?" Most of us have been told off about it in the nursery, and discouraged from doing it. I remember once travelling in the train with a small boy who pointed to the clock in Banbury station and asked, "What does that clock say?" And the mother said, "It's a quarter to two". And the small boy said, "Why is it a quarter to two?" A child like that grows up into a scientist, and spends its whole life asking why. All our science comes from the human habit of asking for the reason of everything, our ineradicable belief that every event must have a cause. And when we've pushed that habit as far as it will go, all we have done is to weave long chains of causes, each one depending on the next. Why did you twist your ankle? Because the low gate into the garden was shut when you didn't expect it to be. Why was it shut? To keep the little pigs out. Why were the little pigs running loose? Because there

wasn't enough feed for them if they were put in a sty.
Why wasn't there enough feed for them? Because
ships get torpedoed in the Atlantic. Why do ships
get torpedoed in the Atlantic? Because we are at
war with Germany. Why are we at war with Germany?
And so on. The series of causes stretches back and
back, and you never get to the end of it. But, you see,
it can't really be infinite. Because an infinite series of
causes all depending on one another wouldn't be a
sufficient explanation of anything. Somewhere, at
the end of that chain, there must be a First Cause
which is not caused by anything which went before it.
And that First Cause is God. His face looks down at
us, as we try to run away from him, looks down this
long avenue of causality, and reminds us that he made
us; we did not make ourselves.

" All right," says the scientist, " we won't talk about
causes and effects, if it has these uncomfortable
consequences. We will content ourselves with observing the pattern of things as we find it in our experience; the wonderful order there is in nature, and
so on." But, you see, that doesn't make them any
better off. Order can only be the expression of a mind;
and who was it that put that order into nature, which
we discover with our scientific instruments? If you
take a razor-blade, and a blade of grass, and put them
under a powerful microscope, you'll find that the edge
of a razor-blade isn't really straight at all; it's all
hopelessly jagged and uneven, so that you can't
imagine why your father doesn't cut himself shaving
every morning instead of just some mornings. But
the blade of grass is still absolutely even all along, not
a dent in it. Now, who did that? Not you or I.

The more we try to map out the pattern of nature, the more are we driven to the conclusion that it exhibits the working of a Mind greater than any human mind. And this creative Mind we have to call God. We have looked along a fresh avenue of experience, and still we see his face looking down at us through the trees.

That's the story we read in the world around us. If we look, instead, at ourselves, at the place we human beings occupy in the universe, it's the same thing. Man asks himself, " What am I here for? The cow is here to give me milk, the sheep are here to give me wool, the bees are here to give me honey—I am here, to give who what? " Have you ever asked yourself, " What am I for? What is the use of my existing? " Perhaps you think you have an easy answer, by saying, " Oh, I exist to keep my mother happy; she'd be frightfully upset if anything happened to me ". Yes, but then, what does she exist for? Don't say, " She exists to keep me happy "; that gets us back into a circle, like that silly game where about a dozen people all sit on one another's knees, number twelve sitting on the knees of number one, and then one falls down and you all fall down. I daresay you know the game; a nice quiet game for the dormitory. If, on the other hand, you say that your mother exists to keep your father happy, then we shall have to ask what he exists for, and so on and on endlessly. In the last resort there must be Somebody for whom, to serve whose purposes, everything else exists; and that Somebody must be God. His face looking at us again, down this new avenue in the forest.

Or perhaps man asks himself, " What is all this

about right and wrong? What do I mean when I say,
It is my duty to do this or that? It isn't, very often,
what *I* want to do; we very seldom refer to duty except
when we are talking of something we don't want to
do. Duty is only an abstract word; are we, living
human beings, going to have our conduct dictated
to us by a mere abstraction? No, the thing which we
don't like not to do, yet isn't our will, must be somebody else's will for us; whose? " In the long run
there must be Somebody whose will is the only thing
that matters, for any human being in the world. And
that Somebody must be God. One more avenue,
and still the same face looking down at us; there is no
getting away from it, whichever way we turn.

God as the First Cause which lies behind all other
causes, God as the Mind which expresses itself in
the pattern of creation, God as the Last End or
Purpose for which everything else exists, God as the
supreme Will which imposes moral duties on mankind—always, you see, if we try to run away from God,
we shall see him in the distance like that, an uncomfortable Fact in the background. But only if we
try to run away from him. . . . If we *want* God, if we
try to find him, then the process is quite easy, and we
find him, not at a distance, but close to us; not an
uncomfortable fact, but a comforting Friend.

You are made up of matter and spirit. Your body,
the thing which is in the way when somebody runs
into you on the stairs, is matter. Your soul, the thing
in you which thinks, the thing in you which loves,
is spirit. Which belongs to a higher order, your body
or your soul? Your soul obviously: it gives you a
richer life than the animals have; your rabbits, for

example, can't do the multiplication table or write home, as you can. Spirit, then, is a higher order than matter; rules it, is the explanation of it. But your spirit doesn't rule the universe, isn't the explanation of the universe; nor is mine, nor is Hitler's. There must be, then, a Spirit which rules this universe of matter, and a Spirit not confined and limited as yours and mine are; that is God. Now, all day long your attention is directed outwards towards the world of matter; your food and the sunshine and the aeroplanes flying overhead. Look inwards instead; look into your own soul; there is God. He is present to your soul, just as the sunshine is present to your body, only much closer. How could it be otherwise? Spirit is not confined by space; therefore distance cannot divide you from God. God is unlimited, therefore he is everywhere; you can't be separated from God. The only thing that divides us from him is the fact that we don't think about him enough, don't love him as we ought to. You don't have to think of him as far away at the end of a long avenue. He's here.

Not believe in God? Of course you do; you couldn't believe in yourself otherwise; you couldn't call your soul your own. And as a rule people who don't believe in God don't believe in themselves, can't call their souls their own; that is how they come to believe in Hitler or some nonsense of that kind. " But," you say, " if the fact of God's existence is so obvious, where is the necessity of believing in it? Surely belief only comes in where there's something you can't prove for yourself, something you have to take on trust? " Well, it's quite true that the Church doesn't expect us to believe in God merely because

Jesus Christ has revealed him to us; the fact that God exists is something, she tells us, which we ought to be able to find out for ourselves. What Jesus Christ has done is to reveal to us more clearly WHAT God is— that he is our Father, for example; we shall have to talk about that next Sunday.

Meanwhile, it's important that we should go on reminding ourselves that we believe in God; not so much because it is difficult to *believe* that he exists as because it is difficult to *realize* that he exists. Our minds turn, don't they, so naturally towards creatures, and away from God. Ever since the Fall the human mind is like a dog's-eared corner in one of your books—you know how one is continually straightening it out, and always finding that it has turned down again by the next time the book is opened. We have been warped out of the straight ever since the Fall; we are always thinking about creatures, about our comforts, about our plans, about our fellow-men, and our minds only travel back to God if we turn them, by a deliberate act, towards him. And so we have got to go on reminding ourselves, " I believe in God ", or we should find it difficult to remember he was there at all. It is such a long time since we thought about him last, and he—he is so quiet about it.

Well, I expect you are still thinking we haven't got very far with the *Credo*. Last week we only managed the words " I believe ", and even this week we've only got as far as " I believe in God "; there's not much to get excited about so far. . . . You're so wrong, if you think that, so absolutely wrong! There couldn't possibly be anything more exciting than the news, " God exists "; it turns everything right round, makes everything fall into place, redresses the balance. What matters is no longer ME, but God. He, not I, is the centre of existence; his will matters, not mine; it is what he thinks about things, what he thinks about people, that makes the difference, not what I think about them; his glory, not my glory, is to be the thing I live for; a hundred years hence, when you and I are dead and gone, it will still matter whether the human race is free or enslaved, is happy or miserable, because there will still be a God reigning in heaven, then as now.

Forgive me, you can't understand all that. Not because you are stupid, but because you are young. When you are young, you can always fall back on yourself for company, unless you are a very melancholy kind of person. When you go to bed at night, and can't get to sleep yet, you can be quite happy thinking about your own plans and your own pleasures, your own friends and your own ambitions; you can lie there day-dreaming, and tell yourself stories about what you are going to do when you grow up, and what sort of man you are going to marry. But when you've had fifty years and more of your own company, it ceases to be quite so enjoyable—you've got bored with it. And that breeds a dreadful loneliness inside the human soul, unless the human soul has learned, and has managed to remember, and still believes, that God exists. You have begun to see yourself as a pretty second-rate sort of article; your prospects of getting your way over this and that don't seem so frightfully important; your judgement of things and of people doesn't seem to matter so much; what the map of Europe will be like in a hundred years' time is a speculation that doesn't much interest you. THEN, to believe that God exists means that you have something—better still, that you have somebody—to fall back upon; everything still matters, because there is God's will to be taken into account, God's glory to be considered. " I BELIEVE IN GOD "; forty years from now, if you keep then the faith you have now, you will be thanking God that God exists.

III

The Father Almighty

UPON MY word, I believe this is the most difficult clause in the whole of the *Credo*. Not theoretically; in theory it slips off your tongue, doesn't it, without giving you a moment's pause for reflection. Our Father, Almighty—of course God is that; when you have said that you have hardly done more than give a definition of what you mean by " God ". Yes, but in real life what is the thing that most of all tempts people to give up their religion? Why, misfortune, especially when it comes upon them suddenly; or when it comes upon them just when they think they have been behaving well, so that God ought to be in a good temper with them; or when it comes upon them simultaneously from every side, so that it looks as if Providence had singled them out specially for its frowns. At such times, people are more swayed by the feelings of the heart than by the reasonings of the brain. A young wife, for example, who has suddenly lost her husband, will say to herself, " Could God have prevented this happening? If not, he is not Almighty. Did God, then, *want* this to happen? If so, he is no Father of mine. Father if you will, but if so, he is powerless to help those who trust in him. Almighty if you will, but if so, he is cruel. One or the other, but not both; an Almighty Father would not treat me like that ".

So what we have got to do this afternoon is first of all to see what we mean by saying God is Almighty, and then to see what we mean by calling him our Father, and then to consider how misfortune comes to us, all the same. And I think we have got our work cut out for us.

God is Almighty in the sense that no limits can be imposed on him by anything outside himself. That follows from what we were saying last Sunday. He is the cause of everything, all movement originates from him; nothing, therefore, can happen unless in some sense he wills it. If there are any limits to his activities, they must be limits imposed by himself, not by somebody or something else. And therefore whatever solution we try to find for the mystery of suffering, there is one answer which evidently gets no marks at all. You mustn't represent God as *powerless* to prevent human suffering; you mustn't think of him as a kind of amiable Official up in heaven who is really very sorry about it, but he's afraid nothing can be done. If you were determined to commit suicide, and (after taking poison) you covered yourself with petrol and set your clothes alight and then jumped from a fourth-storey window, cutting your throat as you did so, God could quite easily save your life if he chose to. I don't suppose for a moment he would want to, so it's not a safe thing to try; but if he chose to, he could.

When we say that God is Almighty, we mean that he can do anything which is not against reason. God couldn't create two equal-sized things one of which was larger than the other. But that isn't to say that he is being hampered by something outside himself. The laws of reason are part of the truth, and the truth is part of himself, or rather is himself; God is truth. God could bring a dead man to life; but, without doing that, he couldn't prevent a dead man's wife being a widow. Unless she married again, of course. All that hasn't much to do with our immediate point; but I thought it might be as well to mention the fact that God can't do things which contradict themselves, because it is a question which occasionally bothers people.

And at the same time God is our Father. " Doubt-less thou art our Father," the Jews used to say, " though Abraham be ignorant of us, and Israel acknowledge us not "; and St. Paul goes so far as to tell us that all earthly fatherhood takes its name from the fatherhood of God; without him there would be no fatherhood at all. The heathen, although they represented their gods as pretty useless sort of people, used to call them " father "; the word JUPITER only means " father up in the sky ". But the notion we have of God's Fatherhood comes chiefly from the teaching of our Lord; " your Father who is in heaven " is a phrase constantly on his lips, and you only need to remember a few familiar verses in order to realize what he means by it. God is our Father in the sense that he knows us intimately; " thy Father who sees what is done in secret "—no shams can take him in. He is interested in everything he has made; a sparrow cannot fall to the ground without his will. He cares for his creatures independently of whether they care for him; he makes his sun to rise on the evil and the good, sends his rain on the just and on the unjust. And his purpose is a beneficent purpose; we cannot always see how, but we must take it on faith. A human father will not give a stone to his son when the son asks for bread; how much more will your heavenly Father give wholesome gifts to those who ask him for them? One of the strongest notes in our Lord's teaching is this emphasis on the way in which we ought to trust God as our Father; the whole of Christianity is built up round it.

But fatherhood, of course, is not a simple term, though it sounds as if it was. Different ages, different periods of civilization, have different ideas about what a father's duties are, what a father's rights are. In the old Roman law *patria potestas*, the father's authority over his children, was a very far-reaching thing; in certain circumstances a father had a right to put his children to death without having any recourse to law. Your father was somebody who had jolly well got to be obeyed. Whereas nowadays we think of a father as a person whose job it is to devote his whole life to giving us treats. He has to throw a hearth-rug over him and come into the room pretending to be a bear, to amuse us when we are small. We are allowed to go into his bedroom and fiddle with his things when he is shaving, a circumstance which has always made me glad that I am a bachelor. He is pathetically anxious to score good marks with his children, by sending them to the cinema three times a week, and so on. You will see, then, that there is a good deal of difference between the ancient idea of a father and the modern idea of a father. Now, which of these ideas ought we to have in mind when we call Almighty God our Father?

I suppose we ought to strike a line somewhere in between the two estimates. After all, though I know you are the wrong people to say it to, there is such a thing as spoiling one's children. I know there is a modern theory of education which makes out that you should never say to a child, " Don't do that ". But when I travel with small children in railway-carriages I am sometimes tempted to think that that sort of thing can be overdone. A father who never says " No " has, commonly, a spoilt child. Think for a moment what that phrase, " a spoilt child ", means. It doesn't just mean that the child grows up a nuisance to its parents. It means that the essential nature of the child is warped, is pushed out of its true pattern, is allowed to go bad, like fruit on a fruit-tree which is not picked in time. If your parents spoil you, you become something like those purple potatoes with holes in them, instead of those nice white or pink potatoes which you put into the basket. It is the job of parents, unless they are rich enough to pay nuns to do it for them, to train their children to alter their nature in the right direction. And God is training you and me. If he gave us absolutely everything we asked for; if you had only to kneel down and say, " Please, God, I want a holiday tomorrow ", and he would always put it into the nuns' heads to give you a holiday next day, for no particular reason, then it would not be long before you would become a spoilt child. You would become very selfish, and unpleasant-ly conceited, and uncommonly lazy. God is altering our natures all the time, is turning us into the kind of people he wants us to be; he wouldn't be our true Father otherwise. That alone would be enough to warn us that, in this imperfect world, we have got to take the rough with the smooth.

I say, " in this imperfect world ", because after all
we are fallen creatures. Our nature, ever since the
Fall, tends to go wrong, and if it is to be saved from
going wrong it has to be saved by discipline, by coming
up against unpleasant things in life as well as pleasant
things. But there is another reason why the Fall makes
the world a more uncomfortable place for you and me
than it was for Adam and Eve in Paradise. God has
given us free will, and that means giving us the
freedom to interfere with one another's lives. I daresay you know the old problem, What would happen
if an irresistible ram met an immovable post? I
don't mean a male sheep, I mean a battering ram.
Well, the answer to that problem is that God couldn't
make an irresistible ram and at the same time make
an immovable post. It's one of the things which, as I
was saying just now, even God can't do, because it is
a contradiction in terms. And in the same way God
can't give us the freedom to hurt one another without
giving us, at the same time, the opportunity to be
hurt. He couldn't give free will to King Herod without putting the Holy Innocents in danger of being
massacred. Of course, you may say that he might
interfere at the last moment, by a miracle if necessary,
to prevent the wickedness of certain human beings
doing harm to other human beings. But obviously
if he always did that, free will would become a farce.
There is bound to be suffering in a fallen world where
human beings have free will, because they will inflict
suffering on one another. To that extent God does
limit his own Almighty power. He lets us do harm to
one another, because if he didn't, the gift of free will
would become meaningless.

" Yes," you say, " that's all very well, but you can't explain all the suffering in the world like that. When you come across a person who has to spend whole years of his or her life bearing the tortures of a painful disease, or when a flourishing town is suddenly turned into a heap of ruins by an earthquake, you can't blame human free will for that. Nobody can be held responsible for tragedies of that kind except the God who is all-powerful—therefore he could have prevented it, who is our Father—therefore he must have wanted to prevent it." But it must be repeated—suffering can be good for us, because it is a discipline we need; it helps to turn us into the kind of people God wants us to be. He wants us to be detached from earthly things, and it would be difficult for us to be like that if we always had our own way. He wants us to learn patience—and how should we learn patience if we had nothing to endure? He wants us to trust him blindly, and the very condition of such trust as that is that we should not know, and should not ask to know, why he treats us as he does. He wants us to be humble, and how should we cultivate humility if our plans always went right? All that we can see, I hope, without much difficulty; but there is more to it than that.

Suffering is a debt which we owe to God in satisfaction for our sins, as the punishment of our sins. He has made us moral beings; and a moral being is distinguished, not merely by having free will, so that he can choose between right and wrong; he is held responsible for the choice, and has to atone for it by punishment if he chooses wrong. God could have heaved you and me up into heaven like so many sacks of coal, but he wasn't going to do that. It would have been unworthy of our dignity as human beings. No, you and I are to settle our score with him, before we get to heaven, by undergoing suffering either in this world or in Purgatory beyond. " You are my child," he says, " and because you are my child, I am not going to treat you as a dumb thing, to be pushed about unwillingly this way and that. Your will is to be made one with mine; and in order that this may happen, your will must accept, from me, the punishment which your sins have deserved. So, when I promote you to the happiness of heaven, there will be no ugly gap between your will and mine, no discrepancy between us that has to be smoothed away. As a punished sinner, you will fit in naturally in an order of things where my will is perfectly obeyed—not otherwise." It isn't easy for us, perhaps, to understand that; but that, I think, is how the Saints would explain it to us.

The Saints, indeed, would tell us more than that. They would tell us that Jesus Christ suffered, and therefore it is an honour for his servants to be allowed to suffer, and unite their sufferings with his, like our Lady standing at the foot of the Cross. They would tell us why it is that it is so often the best people we know, not the most wicked or the most selfish people we know, that have most in the way of hardships to bear. It is because the good people *want* to suffer, want to be like Christ. . . . I am afraid you and I are very far from feeling like that, and whenever we are afflicted with a slight bilious headache we complain that we are being very badly treated. And we think afterwards, " How awful it would be if I had to suffer really cruel pain, through long illness or ill-treatment, when I put up such a poor show over a slight set-back like this!" I hope we may comfort ourselves with this thought; people who have experience in such matters, doctors and nurses and so on, will tell you that on the whole, as a general thing, people who have a great deal to suffer are very good about it; very brave, very unwilling to complain, resigned, more than you would think possible, to the lot which Providence has chosen for them. Let us hope that it will be so with you and me, when the time comes.

God is Almighty, but he couldn't make a world in which people were free to kill one another without making it a world in which people are liable to get killed; that would be inconceivable. God is our Father, but because we are fallen children he disciplines us to prevent us becoming spoilt children; punishes us to make us his children more than ever, because if we accept our punishment we associate ourselves with the atonement which Jesus Christ made for us; more his children than ever, because we win the right to say, when heaven opens for us, " See, Father, I have performed my task of reparation, and here I am ".

IV

Maker of heaven and earth

WHEN WE were discussing the clause, " I believe in God ", I pointed out to you that the world must have been created by God; there was no other account you could give of it. When you turn that sentence the other way round, and say, " God created the world ", you come up against one of the most un- accountable things that could possibly have hap- pened. Why did God want to create the world? From all eternity to all eternity he lives in heaven, utterly self-sufficient; nothing outside himself could possibly contribute to the happiness and to the glory that is his. Why did he want there to be anything else? It's no good telling me that he must have been lonely with nobody to know, nobody to know him, with nobody to love, nobody to love him. Because, you see, the doctrine of the Holy Trinity knocks all that argument on the head. From all eternity the Mind of God produced a Thought; a Thought equal to, and worthy of, itself. That is what we mean by the Divine Word, the second Person of the Blessed Trinity. And in the same instant, between that Divine Mind and that Divine Thought, Love sprang into existence, a Love which flowed back and forth, in perfect measure, between those two. And so a third Person enriches the life of the Godhead, that eternal

Love which we call the Holy Spirit. There is no loneliness, then, imaginable in God's existence; the Divine Life would have full scope for its activities, even if there were nothing else.

No, there is no really satisfactory account of why Creation ever happened. We know that it did, because here we are. But the most the theologians can tell us is that it is the nature of goodness to diffuse itself, so that God uses Creation as a kind of reservoir for the overflow of his inexhaustible love. We can't, after all, form any real picture in our minds of what we mean by " creating ". You and I never make anything; we only rearrange things that are there already. You didn't really *make* a rabbit hutch; you only got hold of an old umbrella-stand or something and smashed it up and put the bits together again; you didn't MAKE anything that wasn't there before. But when God made heaven and earth there was nothing there before; God simply called them into existence. Perhaps the nearest we can get to imagining what the act of creation means is to think of a person writing a poem, say, or a book. I don't know whether any of you write poems yet; but if you do you will know what I mean. It isn't like taking a piece of French and turning it into a piece of English; or taking one set of figures and dividing them by another and getting a third set of figures and writing " Ans." after them. No, when you have written a poem, something, you feel, has come into existence; English literature is richer than it was before, though perhaps not much richer than it was before. When God creates, something which had only been a thought in his mind takes shape on the canvas of real existence.

And perhaps that comparison makes it a little easier for us to understand *why* God created anything. I mean, when you wrote your poem, it wasn't exactly that you *wanted* to write the poem; the poem (so to speak) wanted to be written. The guinea-pig (or whatever it was) affected your fancy in such a way that you couldn't feel happy until the poem *was* written. When you showed it to a friend, that was perhaps vanity on your part; and when you write your first novel, and send it to somebody who is very busy already, with a note saying, " I enclose a novel in 856 type-written pages, I wonder if you would mind just reading through it and telling me whether you think it is any good "—that will probably mean a certain amount of vanity on your part. But merely *getting the thing down on paper* isn't vanity; it's just the craving for self-expression. God can't have a craving for anything; but perhaps we may compare that overflowing of his goodness which resulted in creation, very distantly, to what happens when an author simply " has " to write.

" Maker of heaven and earth "—does heaven mean just the sky and the stars and so on? I don't think so; the Nicene Creed, the *Credo* we say at Mass, calls God " the Creator of heaven and earth, of all things visible and invisible "; and I imagine that here, too, " heaven " means the supernatural order, the world which we can't see, even through a telescope. You see, when we said " I believe in God ", we were letting ourselves in for rather more than we bargained for. There had to be a God to explain our existence and the existence of the world we see around us. But when God revealed himself to us, he explained that this world we see around us isn't the whole of his creation, isn't nearly the whole of his creation. It's only a tiny corner of it, hardly worth mentioning. When you see an iceberg in the Atlantic it looks like a sort of mound of ice floating on the top of the water. But really there is much, much more of the iceberg floating under the water, which you don't see. So it is with God's creation; we see just the tip of it, as it were, a few million stars among which our planet is rather insignificant. Underneath all that and supporting all that is a supernatural world we can't see. We only know about it from revelation, and even so, very little.

God has just lifted up a corner of the curtain, and given us a peep behind it, very much as one gives a small child a peep into the room where the Christmas tree is, to satisfy its curiosity, before the actual event comes off. We just know that there are angels, pure spirits with no body, who serve God day and night, and who are looking after us all the time; that there are fallen angels, God's enemies and ours; that there is a heaven for us to win, a hell for us to avoid, a Purgatory for us to get through with as little of delay as possible. Having shown us that much, God lets the curtain fall again, and says, " You'll have plenty of time to look at all that later on ".

I say, we only know about these things by revelation. But of course our unaided reason might have guessed that there was something of the kind. If God was going to create, why should he create nothing except material things which you and I could see out of two holes in our face? If he was going to make you and me who have both souls and bodies, and guinea-pigs which have bodies but no souls, wasn't it to be expected that he should make other beings which have souls (or rather spirits) but no bodies? And that is what the angels are.

At the same time, all this talk of an invisible world does make one feel rather uncomfortable. Creation seemed rather a cosy sort of affair when it just meant God and your soul and the world of matter. The world of matter might be very vast; there might be systems on systems of planets much bigger than ours, but that didn't matter much, because, after all, planets haven't got souls. The planet Venus may be much bigger than you, but after all it's you who have the advantage, because you can point up in the sky and say, " That's the planet Venus ", whereas the planet Venus can't point down at you and say, " That's Mary Jane ". But when you read about the holy Angels, " Ten thousand times ten thousand ministered unto him ", and so on, it does make you feel rather small. God, you feel, can't have much need of Mary Jane when he has got all these cherubim and seraphim to pay him worship. Creation, instead of being a cosy little affair, has become a large, draughty sort of place in which you feel lost. And you almost wish that when God set about creating things, he hadn't done it on such a magnificent scale. You would like to be rather more in the centre of the stage instead of being given a walk-on part.

Well, we've got to keep a sense of proportion about all that. And I think the main thing to remember is this—that your soul is a special creation. When a fresh guinea-pig comes into existence, God doesn't have to create anything exactly; I think that is the implication in the first chapter of Genesis, where God says to the fishes and the birds and the beasts, " Increase and multiply ", as if he meant, " I'm not going to go on creating fresh guinea-pigs ". And that's how your body came into existence. But your soul, you see, is quite different; you didn't get that from your parents. God created it specially, for your body; created it out of nothing, just as he created the worlds. He wasn't bound to do that. It's true, it would have been very awkward if he hadn't, because that would have meant a human being without a soul, a thing which has never happened yet! But it was his *will* to create you; his eternal goodness overflowed again, this time into you. He thought of you specially, and he still thinks of you specially, just as much as if he had no angels to worship him and to serve him.

Let's remember this, though : that when you create something it belongs to you. If you wrote a poem, and I found it lying about, and sent it up to the *Tablet* signed R. A. Knox, and got some money for it, you could bring an action against me at law. And because God created you, you belong absolutely to God. If one of your friends says, " You might give me half that apple ", it is possible for you to reply, " I shall please myself about that ". I don't mean that that is a very nice way of putting it, but you are within your rights. But if God tells you he wants you to do something, or wants you not to do something, it's terrible that you should reply, " I shall please myself about that ". God owns you; he is what you are for; to do his will is something that ought to come much more naturally to you than doing your own will. And however much he may interfere in your life, God is within his rights. If you have written a poem in which

you've called the guinea-pig a funny pig, and then you
come to the conclusion that that isn't a very good
rhyme, and you change it to " skinny pig ", you are
within your rights; it's your poem, and you can alter
it if you want to. Just so God made you what you are,
made the framework in which your life is to be lived;
and if (say) he allows a person who was once rich
to become poor, or a person who was once beautiful
to be disfigured by an accident, he is only doing what
he has a right to do; the Lord gave, and the Lord
hath taken away, blessed be the name of the Lord.

Meanwhile, I hope you won't ask me to tell you why
God has made heaven and earth as he has made them
and not somehow else. I'm not here to answer the
question, Why did God make ear-wigs? or the
question, Couldn't God have made the wart-hog
rather more presentable while he was about it? We
aren't, it seems to me, in any position to answer
questions like that. In the first place, because we
don't know what kind of place the world would have
been if Adam hadn't fallen—or, if you like to put it in
that way, what kind of place the world would have
been if God hadn't, when he created Adam, foreseen
Adam's fall. The account of the Fall in Genesis
definitely seems to imply that the thorns and briers
which give such trouble to the farmer and the
gardener weren't meant to be there originally, or
weren't meant to be so uncommonly vigorous and
difficult to get rid of. For all I know, in an unfallen
world there wouldn't have been any ear-wigs. But
quite apart from these theological speculations, it's
very difficult, merely as a matter of human philosophy,
to supply alternative programmes for the kind of

world God might have made if he hadn't made this one. If you sit down and try to do it, with a pencil and a piece of paper, I think you will find your proposed world is either something very tame or something very fantastic. All you can say is that God has made a world rich in variety; and a world in which a whole lot of species that used to exist, like the mammoth or the dodo, have been allowed to die out. All of which suggests to my mind the profusion of fancy which you would expect from a great artist; there is a sort of splendid carelessness about creation as we know it which almost seems meant to remind us —you get that worked out in the book of Job—that God's thoughts are not as our thoughts, and his workmanship does not abide the question of critics with limited minds like yours and mine.

Meanwhile, God has made heaven and earth *for you*. Whether things present, or things to come, St. Paul says, all are yours. We live in this world surrounded by his creatures, and by creatures I don't mean earwigs or guinea-pigs specially, but the whole of our life here and the opportunities it gives us. Creatures exist to remind us of God and make us think how much greater the Maker must be than the things he has made; how much more irresistible his power must be than the power of the whirlwind, how much more captivating his beauty must be than the beauty of the sunset. Creatures exist so that we can enjoy them and be grateful for them; so that when we have had a holiday we can go to bed thanking God, with a glow in our hearts, for all his goodness to us. Creatures exist so that we may make a right and wise use of them, mortifying ourselves and disciplining our appetites instead of being selfish about them, and making pigs of ourselves over them.

All that is true of God's earthly creatures; but meanwhile, God made heaven as well as earth, and not only earth, but heaven, is ours, is meant for us to enjoy. Even now, the protection of the holy angels and the prayers of our Blessed Lady and all the Saints are available to us, because we are his children. How much more thrilling it will be when one day, please God, we put Purgatory behind us, and find, in heaven, the end for which we were really created, the existence which really satisfies the longings of our nature! Only then will the Artist put the finishing touches to his work; only then shall we be able to admire the grand scale of it, the perfect symmetry of it. The curtain will be drawn aside, and the Author of all that exists will stand there to take our applause.

V

And in Jesus Christ

Now WE'VE got to the real centre of the *Credo*; this
is what the *Credo* is about. We oughtn't, you know,
to hurry over the words JESUS CHRIST, as if it was all
one word. When we give a person two names, we may
mean any one of three things. The extra name may
be merely, so to speak, for ornament. When you are
christened, it's all right for you to be christened by
one name, say Mary. But if your godfathers and god-
mothers prefer it, you can be christened Mary Jane
Maude Blanche Sophia Ludmilla Emerentiana
Beatrice Rose; there's no extra charge for it. And all
those names are simply different ways of describing
the same person. If somebody walking behind you
shouts " Mary! " you jump, and if they shout
" Jane! " you jump; that's all there is to it. Or,
sometimes, the extra name is added by way of
distinguishing one person from another. You may talk
about William the Conqueror to distinguish that
William from all the other Williams who weren't
conquerors; or you may talk about Jack the Giant-
killer simply to distinguish him from Jack and the
Beanstalk. But sometimes when you call a person by
two names, or by a name and a title—it all comes to
the same thing—you are really conveying some information about them. You may say, " That's Mr.

Davis, the postman ", by way of explaining why he's
wandering about the drive, because Mr. Davis doesn't
always wear uniform. Or you may say, " That's Mary
Snooks ", by way of conveying the information that
that is the daughter of the famous film star, Mr.
Snooks. A name may be a mere ornament, or it may
be a mere label, or it may tell you something about the
person it is applied to.

Now when we talk about " Jesus Christ ", it is not
(though we often think it is) an elaborate way of talking
about our Lord, when you might just have said
" Jesus " or " Christ " instead. And it is not a mere
way of distinguishing him from the famous Israelite
general who conquered Palestine, whose name was
also Jesus, although we usually call him Josue. No,
when we say " Jesus Christ " we are not merely
naming our Lord, we are saying something about him.
" Christ " is not really a name; it is a title. And these
two words are the real centre of the Credo, because
when the holy Apostles first went out to preach the
Christian religion these two words contained the whole
substance of their message. They went about telling
their Jewish friends, " Jesus is the Christ ". And their
Jewish friends knew what they meant by it.

If you don't know what they meant by it, that's
because you haven't read a great deal of the Old
Testament. Where had we got to when we left off
last Sunday? " I believe in God, the Father Almighty,
Maker of heaven and earth." Now God might have
left it at that; that might, but for his mercy, have
been absolutely all that we know about him. It's
all that our unaided reason could tell us. If we are
not to depend on our unaided reason, what is it that

is going to help us? Why, revelation. So, now that
we've found out everything we could find out about
God by the use of our unaided reason, let's look round
and make sure that he hasn't revealed himself. That
will mean going back, won't it, over history? We've
got to take a good, comprehensive view of history,
and by that I don't mean English history, Alfred and
the cakes and so on; we've got to look at the history
of the world.

When you come to do that, you find that there's
one race in the world which seems quite unique; I
mean the Jews. It stands alone in all sorts of ways;
what other race, starting from such a small bit of
territory, has so overspread the world? What other
race remains so unchanged in its characteristics all
through the centuries; what other race is so little
affected by contact with its neighbours? What other
race has won so few conquests, yet had such a profound influence upon history? The Jews, whatever
way you take them, are unlike anybody else. And this,
I think, is one of their most curious characteristics—
the Jew dreams of the future, not of the past; he is
always looking forward to a good time coming,
instead of moaning about the good old times in the
past.

In our own day, that doesn't seem very surprising
to us, because we have all come to believe in a thing
called progress, which seems to mean that the world
is getting better and better all the time. But that, you
know, is a quite modern idea; it was only invented, I
think, late in the eighteenth century by a priest. I
wonder what he thinks about it now? Before that, the
tendency everywhere in the world was to say that the

good old times were over, and we should never see the like of that again. You get it as far back as Homer, when you might have expected the world to be still feeling pretty young. Somebody like Diomede in the *Iliad* will pick up a stone and throw it at the next man, "the kind of stone", Homer tells you, "which three men would find it hard to lift, the sort of measly specimens you find about nowadays, but Diomede managed it quite easily all by himself". That you find all through classical literature, they're always telling you how splendid it used to be in the golden age, the age of Saturn, when people used to lie about under trees eating acorns, and never went to war with one another. But it's not like that in Hebrew literature —and we've got a great deal of Hebrew literature to study, remember, the whole of the Old Testament. The Jew knew perfectly well that man had lost his Paradise; there it was written down for him in the third chapter of Genesis. But he didn't go round moaning about it; that's the curious thing. "Behold, the days come, saith the Lord"—that is the keynote of Hebrew literature. They are always looking hopefully to the future, instead of looking back regretfully on the past.

Well, let's take a bird's-eye view of the history of this extraordinary people. It begins with the patriarchs, Abraham, Isaac and Jacob. You know them by name, and you have seen fancy pictures of them; you imagine Abraham as an old man in purple, looking rather as if he had thrown the window-curtain round him dressing up for charades, who always went for a walk with a stick in one hand and a thurible in the other. I don't think he really looked like that; he was just a tough old desert chief who had settled down to pasture his herds in Chanaan, with about three hundred clansmen obeying his orders; outwardly just like any of the local chiefs round there. But if you had met Abraham, this would have struck you about him, that the old man lived in the future. He would tell you God had promised to give the whole land of Chanaan to his descendants; more than that, God had promised that in his posterity all the nations of the earth should be blessed.

That dream he handed on to his son Isaac, and Isaac to his son Jacob. Jacob, at the end of his life, emigrated with all his family to Egypt, and was much better off there, with a royal grant of some of the best grazing-lands. But when he died, he made his children swear that his bones should be taken back, sooner or later, to the land of Chanaan. To him, too, it was a holy land, this parched strip of the Levantine coast; he wouldn't be buried anywhere else; it was going to be important one day.

His descendants grew unpopular in Egypt. They were reduced to slavery, and set to work building the pyramids. Moses, their great national hero, set them free from this bondage and led them out into the Arabian desert; at the end of forty years they settled down in, and conquered, the same land of Chanaan in which their ancestors had been rather insignificant cattle-owners. Just before he died, Moses made a curious remark. He said that, one day, God would raise up a prophet like himself; to him, said Moses, you must really listen. And from that day onward the Jews were always expecting a prophet to appear who would be a second Moses. And they did have great prophets, Elias and Eliseus and all the rest, but never for a moment did they think that *the* prophet had come. No, *the* prophet was somebody who was going to save Israel, to deliver them from their enemies, as Moses had.

Well, time went on, and the Jews thought they would like to have a king. Their first king wasn't a great success; but the second one, King David, became their great national hero. Now here's a curious thing—in all the poetry he wrote, and all the poetry which was written, it may be, by imitators of his, he was only treated as being of importance for one reason. In his family, years later, a King was to arise who was to be a much greater King than David; he was going to rule from one end of the earth to the other. When a king was crowned, in those days, he was anointed with oil; and so they called this great King who was to become the Messiah, the Anointed One. Afterwards, when the Jews learned to talk Greek, as I hope you all will, they translated that into Greek, and the Greek for the Anointed One is CHRISTOS. And from then onwards the Jews didn't simply look forward to a prophet who was to deliver them, they looked forward to a King who was going to rule the world, a King descended from the family of David, and called the Christ.

King David lived in the time of Homer, or thereabouts; what we call, for our own private reasons, a thousand years B.C. Those thousand years that followed were difficult ones for the Jews. The earthly kingdom of the Jews wasn't a great success; they were always getting invaded by powerful armies from Assyria and Babylon, and in the end the whole people, more or less, were carried away into exile. Even when

they came back from exile, about five hundred years
B.C., they found themselves a very insignificant sort
of nation, compared with what they used to be. All
through that period the chief figures in Jewish
literature were what we call the prophets. The
prophets—there it is again, you see. They didn't sit
about saying, " How much better things used to be
in the time of King David and King Solomon! "
No, they still looked to the future; still said, " How
splendid things will be when the Christ comes to
deliver us! "

And from what the prophets said, flashes here and
there, because the prophets aren't very easy to understand, the Jews learnt a lot they hadn't realized before.
They found out that the reason why they were always
being defeated by their enemies was because they
were so wicked; they didn't keep God's law, they
oppressed the poor, they worshipped false gods, and
so on. And they came to see that the Christ would
have to deliver them, not from their enemies, but from
their sins; that his reign was going to be a reign of
peace and of justice, not a sort of bank holiday which
they would spend in crowing over their enemies. And
there was a strange story—that part of it they found
very difficult to understand—that this King, this
Christ who was to come, would have to suffer, would
have to make atonement for the sins of his people.
And at the same time it began to be clear that this
King, this Christ, was not to be an ordinary human
being. He was somebody who was coming down from
heaven, to judge the world; he would look, the
prophets said, like a Son of Man—which meant, of
course, that he wouldn't just *be* an ordinary son of

man, or what would be the point of saying that he looked like one? By this time, you see, the hopes of the Jews had grown rather confusing, but they were as strong as ever. And round about the year which we call, for our own private reasons, the year Nought, you find pious Jews described as people who waited for the consolation of Israel; they were expecting the Christ to come, because it was about the time the prophet Daniel had foretold that he would.

Do you know what it is to be trying to open a drawer, and going through a bunch of keys, to see if you can find one which will fit? And how splendid it is when at last one of the keys fits in, as if it had been made for that drawer, and the lock turns without difficulty? So it was here; a key fitted the lock; an event happened which corresponded with all that the Jews had been looking forward to. A baby was born in Bethlehem, the son of a poor woman, who called him JESUS. She was poor, but she was descended from King David; and that got known, so that blind beggars, when he grew up, used to shout after him, " Have mercy on us, thou Son of David ". He didn't call himself the Son of David; he used to call himself the Son of Man; to remind people of that Son of Man who was expected to come in judgement. And he claimed to be a prophet, like Moses—greater than Moses, or how could he say, " Moses said this, but I tell you that "? And when he asked his friends who they thought he was, the most intimate of them said, " Thou art the Christ ".

He wouldn't let them tell anybody about it at the time; but later, when the chief priests brought him to trial, and asked him, " Art thou the Christ? " he said,

" I am; and when you see me again, I shall be coming to earth in judgement ". The Son of Abraham, the Son of David, calling himself the Son of Man, claiming to be greater than the prophets, claiming that he had come to found a kingdom, claiming to be the Christ, the Judge of the world—that was Jesus of Nazareth. And because we believe in that claim, we say, " Jesus is the Christ ". The baby who was born at Bethlehem is that Christ, that Anointed One from heaven, whom the Jews had been looking forward to all those centuries. The Key had fitted in the lock, and the door swung open, and revealed to us all we wanted to know about the supernatural world, and heaven. and hell, and the forgiveness of our sins.

VI

His only Son

I DON'T know if you remember what we were saying
in the second of these sermons I've been preaching
to you about the *Credo*. I don't see any reason why
you should; after all, it's a very long time ago; it must
be nearly a month and a half ago, and that's a very long
time to expect you to remember anything. So let me
remind you that we were talking, then, about believing
in God; about how some people, when they are in
great distress of mind or when, unhappily, they have
fallen into sin, try to forget about God; and about how
God won't let them forget him, because everything
in his creation goes on shouting out to them, " No,
God exists ". And it made us think of that impressive
scene in the third chapter of Genesis, where Adam
and Eve, after they have fallen into the sin of dis-
obedience, try to hide themselves from the presence
of God, among the trees of the garden. And of course,
that doesn't work. It isn't long before they hear the
voice of the Lord God calling out, " Adam, where art
thou? " You see, we are God's children; and if it isn't
very irreverent to put it like this—I hope it's not
irreverent—he does for us what grown-up people do
for children: he plays hide-and-seek with us. That
story in Genesis only gives us a kind of fancy picture,
I suppose, of what really happened; because God is

46

everywhere, and sees everything; he doesn't really have to go about hunting for people among the bushes, as you and I do when people hide themselves. But that was the best way for us to understand what happened after man fell; this fancy picture which the Bible has given us of eternal God treating us as grown-up people treat children, playing a game of hide-and-seek.

Well, you don't need to be reminded what happens at hide-and-seek when the person who has hidden has been found. It's the turn of the other person, the person who was seeking before to hide this time. And God is so awfully good to us that he would keep to the rules of the game. Man had tried to hide from God, and God had found him. And now God hid from man, and man had got to try and find him. How was it that God hid himself? We were talking about that last Sunday. He came and hid himself as a little Child, lying on his Mother's breast in a dark cave, in a very unimportant little town called Bethlehem, somewhere in Judea. That was a pretty good way to hide, wasn't it? And of course we men are awfully stupid compared with God. So, for fear we should be too stupid to find him, he did what grown-up people do on such occasions: he gave himself away—gave us hints all over the place. That was what the prophets were for. " Behold, a Virgin shall conceive, and bear a Son. . . . And thou, Bethlehem, in the land of Juda, art not the least among the cities of Juda. . . . The ox knoweth his owner, and the ass his master's crib. . . . A branch shall come up from the root of Jesse "—Jesse was the father of King David—" and thus a flower shall spring from

that root "; hints like that made us prepared to go and
look for a child, born of David's family, at Bethlehem.
" Go on," said the prophets, " you're getting warm."
And then a star appeared to the Wise Men in the East,
and that was better still. " Go on," said the star,
" you're getting warmer." And then an angel appeared to the shepherds, and told them about a child
lying in a manger, and that made it too easy for words.
" Go on," said the angel, " you're getting boiling hot
now." And so the secret was given away; stupid as
we were, we could hardly fail to find out where God
was hiding after that.

Well, what did God do all that for? In the first
place, as we were saying, because he wanted to reveal
himself; because he wanted to tell us more about
himself than we should ever have been able to guess
by the use of our unaided reason. But, remember,
there was another purpose he had in view as well.
Man had sinned; he had been shut out of Paradise,
and he would never find his way back to Paradise
again unless atonement was made for his sin. At
least, when I say that, I'm not being quite accurate.
It was not, in the strict sense, NECESSARY that atonement should be made; God could have said, " Very
well, if you will say you are sorry, I will forgive you ".
But he preferred not to do it like that; he preferred
that atonement should be made in full. You know how
it is when you've done something very unkind to somebody you are really very fond of; you don't want
merely to go and say you're sorry, you want to *do*
something to make up for it. You've got into a temper
with your mamma and called her names; and so you
wait till she isn't looking, and go out and feed the hens

to save her trouble, or you buy her a mug with A
PRESENT FROM BRIDGNORTH written on it—you do
something to *make up* for the beastly way in which
you've treated her. That's what atonement means.
And God decided that the sins of mankind should be
not merely forgiven, but atoned for; something should
be done to make up for them. And that, if you come
to think of it, wasn't easy.

You see, theologians will tell you that the greatness
of an offence is measured by the dignity of the person
against whom the offence is committed; whereas when
it comes to making reparation for an offence the greatness of the reparation is measured by the dignity of
the person who is making it. That isn't really as
difficult as it sounds. You see, if you put out your
tongue at the girl who sits next you in class, it isn't
a ladylike thing to do, but it doesn't matter frightfully.
But if you should so forget yourself, which I hope you
never will, as to put out your tongue at Mother
Margaret, that would be a dreadful thing to do. And
what is the reason of the difference? Why, that
Mother Margaret is a very much more important
person than the girl who sits next you in class. The
offence is measured by the dignity of the person against
whom it is committed. Whereas when it comes to
making reparation it is the other way round. Let's
suppose, for example, that Hitler had wanted to make
peace, and we stated what our terms were, and one
of our peace terms was that Hitler should walk all
the way from London to Birmingham carrying a large
sandwich-board with the words I AM A CAD written
on it. And then, suppose Hitler wrote back and said,
" What about Goering doing that London to

Birmingham walk? Wouldn't that do as well?" We
should have said, "No, of course it wouldn't do as
well. We don't want Cad No. 2, we want Cad No.
1 ". Hitler was a more important person than Goering,
therefore reparation made by Goering wouldn't be as
good as reparation made by Hitler. The greatness of
the reparation is measured by the dignity of the person
who offers it.

Now apply that principle to the question of man's
sin, and the atonement for man's sin. Whom did man's
sin offend? God. Then the offence of man's sin must
be measured by God's dignity. How great is God's
dignity? Infinite. Therefore the reparation made for
man's sin will have to be infinite. But if man makes
that reparation, it will have to be measured by man's
dignity. How great is man's dignity? Finite. Therefore, you see, the sum won't work out. If all the human
beings that have ever existed were to make all the
reparation in their power, that reparation would still
be finite. And reparation which is finite can't make up,
in full, for an offence which is infinite.

Who is there that can offer infinite reparation?
Only he whose dignity is infinite; only God. God
knew that; and he said, "Very well, I will send my
only Son. He shall make reparation ". God's only
Son is the Second Person of the Blessed Trinity, who
himself is God. " God was in Christ, reconciling the
world to himself."

So God became man. He became man in order to
suffer; you can't make atonement for sin without
suffering. And God's nature is impassible, incapable
of suffering; if the Son of God was to atone for us,
he had to become man. What do we mean when we

say, " God became man "? Do we mean that he took upon himself the *appearance* of a man? Do we mean that when the shepherds worshipped at Bethlehem there wasn't really any baby in the manger, it was only a sort of phantom, and God made our Lady and the shepherds and everybody think there was a real baby there? No, that won't do, because where does the suffering come in? When that baby cried, it was because he really felt hungry; just as, thirty-three years later, he was really thirsty when he cried out on the Cross, " I thirst ". No, if Jesus Christ is to atone for us, Jesus Christ must be really man, suffering as we men suffer.

What *do* we mean, then? Do we mean that our Lady gave birth to a man, Jesus Christ, just a man and nothing more? And that afterwards God came and took up his abode in this man's soul, as he does in yours and mine when we receive him in Holy Communion? Only in this man he took up his abode so fully, so specially, that it was possible to call this man the Son of God? No, that won't do either. The man, however much God might dwell in him, wouldn't *be* God. And if he was only man, not God, then, however much he might suffer, the merits of his sufferings would be finite, not infinite. And we wanted infinite satisfaction, you remember, to atone for the infinite offence of man's sin. Jesus Christ, the Baby born at Bethlehem, has got to be man, or he couldn't suffer. And he has got to be God, or the value of his sufferings for us wouldn't be infinite. That is why we have to say, " Jesus Christ was both God and man ".

Well, if you remember all I've been saying to you these last few Sundays, you'll have an objection to

make there. You'll interrupt me by reminding me
that I told you God couldn't do things which are
inconceivable; he couldn't make a thing, for example,
which was at the same time round and square. How,
then, could a Being exist who was both God and Man?
The answer to that is, that we have to make a dis-
tinction. Jesus Christ was both human and Divine,
but in different ways. His nature was human, his
person was Divine. That is what we mean by the
Hypostatic Union. When we say the Litany of the
Sacred Heart, we say, " Heart of Jesus, hypostatically
united to the word of God ", not knowing very much
what it means. Hypo is something you use for
developing photographs, and statics are a kind of
higher mathematics; but all that doesn't help us
much. Hypostatically united means personally united.
It means that Jesus Christ has a human nature, but
in person he is Divine.

A Divine Person with a human nature—and therefore a Divine Person with two natures, one human and
one Divine. Our Lord couldn't stop being God when
he became man. He was still reigning, as God, in
heaven, when our Lady was wrapping him up in his
swaddling-clothes at Bethlehem. You say, " That's
very confusing ". I should just think it was. Nothing
I can suggest in the way of illustration can really be
of any use, simply because the Hypostatic Union is
something unlike anything else in existence; it is a
closer, more intimate union than anything we can
imagine. Our Lady is united to God by love; how
close that bond is! But in the Incarnation you have
a union closer than love itself. The same person on
earth may hold two different positions, two different

titles; as the King was both King of England and Emperor of India; but in the Incarnation it is not a question of two different titles, two different positions; it is a question of two natures, two modes of being. You read stories sometimes of people possessed by devils, and having to be exorcised; and in those stories it seems as if the devil managed to take complete control of the possessed person, spoke with his voice, looked out of his eyes, thought with his mind. But always, even in such a case as that, the human personality is there, must be there, even though it's driven (so to speak) into a corner. But in the Incarnate Christ, though there is a human mind, a human soul, there is no human personality. The Person you see at Bethlehem or on Calvary is God. Nothing in our human experience can be used to illustrate that mystery. But it is a mystery, not a contradiction.

You'll find as you grow up, and get talking to Protestants more and find out what they think about religion, that they are nearly all wrong about what we've been saying this afternoon. They will start by telling you that they believe our Lord was God, but when you question them a little more closely you'll find that most of them think he was a very good man, so good that he was allowed (I'm going to be irreverent again) to enjoy a kind of honorary rank as God. Some of them think it happened when he was baptized, if you remember, in the Jordan, and the Holy Ghost came down on him there in the form of a dove. That, they will tell you, is when our Lord started to be God. But, you see, it's all nonsense really.

If the Baby who lay in the crib at Bethlehem was a human person, then it was a human person who hung on the Cross, and your sins and mine have never been properly atoned for, if that's so, because human sin is an infinite offence to the majesty of God, and you can't atone for an infinite offence by a finite act of reparation. No, God's only Son, wishing to make reparation in full for our fault, took a human nature upon him, because that was the only way in which it was possible for him to suffer. It was like the action of some rich man who makes himself responsible for the debts of a bankrupt, because he thinks those debts ought to be paid. Like that, only different from that, because the condescension was much greater, because the price he paid cost him much more, it cost him his life. "Greater love hath no man than this," he tells us, "that a man should lay down his life for his friends." No *man*, but, being God, he revealed to us a love even greater than the love he spoke of. Being God, he took a human life in order to be able to lay it down; and to lay it down for us, who were not his friends, but his enemies.

VII

Our Lord

WE GET so accustomed to the words which we use in
saying our prayers that we are apt to forget where the
use of them came from; forget, therefore, in a sort of
way, what they mean. Why is it, for example, that
Almighty God is so often referred to as " the Lord "
in the Psalms; and why is it that if we want to allude
casually to the Incarnate Son of God we refer to him
as " our Lord "? The origin of the habit is a rather
curious one.

The Jews had a name for their God; he was called
Jehovah; or rather, the scholars tell us, he was called
Yahweh. But a feeling grew up among them that this
word, Yahweh, was too sacred a thing to be read out
loud. So when they read aloud they substituted for
it the word " Lord ", which was the sort of word
one used when one was talking to a king, and on state
occasions like that—wives used to call their husbands,
" my lord ", a thing they very seldom do nowadays.
And it's a curious thing that we have the same instinct;
only to us the holy name isn't the name of Yahweh,
it's the name of Jesus. Although we use the holy name
of Jesus freely enough in our prayers, when it comes to
ordinary conversation we don't quite like to use it;
it sticks in our throat. So, if we are looking through a
book of pictures, we say, " That's a picture of our Lord

driving the traders out of the temple "; and if somebody said, " That's a picture of Jesus driving the
traders out of the temple ", we should probably find
it was somebody who wasn't a Catholic and perhaps
wasn't a Christian at all. We've got into the habit
of using the phrase " our Lord " merely as a more
reverent way of referring to Jesus, and therefore we
are apt not to reflect what the phrase " our Lord "
really means.

What I want you to see is that this title of Lord
had an everyday, common-or-garden meaning for
the Jews in the Old Testament and even for Christians
in the New Testament, whereas it hasn't got any
such meaning for us. You said "Adonai ", " my
Lord ", not only when you were talking to a king,
but when you were talking to any important person;
for example, a prophet. Servants used it regularly in
addressing their masters, and, as I say, wives in addressing their husbands. Sons used it in addressing
their fathers, though apparently not always. I hope
you remember the parable of the man who said to
his two sons, each of them in turn, " Go and work
in my vineyard ". One of them, if you remember,
said, " I go, Sir ", and went not. The other said
" I will not ", but afterwards he repented and went.
You see, the one who isn't really fond of agriculture
wants to get the right side of his father and put him in
a good temper, so he calls him " Sir ", or " Lord "—
it's all the same word in Greek. And when St. Mary
Magdalen met our Lord in the garden after his resurrection, and mistook him for the gardener, she said,
" Sir ", or " Lord ", " if thou hast carried him hence
tell me where thou hast laid him ". She didn't know

she was talking to her Lord; she was merely trying to put the gardener in a good temper. So that when a Jew in the Old Testament, or a Christian in the New Testament, started saying his prayers, and began them with the word " Lord ", he was using everyday language, though in a special sense. He was addressing the King of all the earth by a title which you used in talking to kings, the Spouse of his soul by a title which wives used in talking to their husbands, the eternal Father by a title sons used in talking to their fathers, the Giver of all good things by the title you used in talking to a stranger, if you wanted to get something out of him. The word wasn't just a form of address; it meant something to him.

But with us, if you come to think of it, it's quite different. We don't address our fellow men as " lord " except on ceremonial occasions, when we are using ceremonious language, a survival from the past. In a court of law the learned counsel will address the judge as " melud "; but he doesn't think of the judge as his lord, really, any more than the judge really thinks of the counsel as learned. And in the same way when you are talking to a bishop it's polite to call him " my lord " now and again—not too often, because it gets tiresome; but you only do it with an effort, and probably get rather flustered about it. Like the boy in buttons in the very old story you probably know, who was carefully coached about saying " my lord " when the bishop came to stay; but when he knocked at the bishop's door next morning, and the bishop said " Who's that? " he forgot about saying " The boy, my lord ", and said " The lord, my boy " by mistake. So that when we come to say our prayers, and start, " Lord, please give me a better report this term ", the word " Lord " doesn't convey any definite meaning to us; it's just a vague title which we use, in a general spirit of humility, to Somebody who is much more important and much more august than we are. It doesn't remind us in any way of the encounters of everyday life.

Living in the twentieth century, living in the Western part of the world, and not under a totalitarian government, we have all gone so frightfully democratic that the idea of having a lord in the literal sense, that is in the sense of being owned by somebody else, has become quite strange, quite foreign to us. We've all read about Sir Walter Raleigh putting his nice new cloak down in the mud so that Queen Elizabeth shouldn't dirty her shoes; that seemed all right to him, because she was the Queen and he was her subject. But you wouldn't find Lord Woolton, for example, putting down his new overcoat for the queen to walk on; he might, I mean, but I don't think it's likely, unless he was very well off for coupons at the moment. And you hear people singing that Indian love-lyric in which the lady tells her husband she is less than the dust beneath his chariot wheels, but you wouldn't find an English wife talking like that; she'd be much more likely to tell her husband to go out and clean the car.

So we don't find it easy now to get a line on the meaning of the word *Lord* by thinking of a king's relation to his subjects, or of a husband's relation to his wife. But, you see, the thing goes further than that. The Latin word for *Lord*, which (as you perhaps know) is *Dominus*, meant, literally, the owner of slaves. And

the immediate picture which the word called up to the
early Christians, many of whom were slaves themselves, was that of a master who really owned you,
owned human beings just as he owned his cattle and
sheep. We don't find it easy to put ourselves back in
the atmosphere of the ancient world, where the master
had a perfect right to kill his slaves if he wasn't satisfied with the way they cooked the dinner. But that
is what *Dominus* meant when the title of *Dominus*
was first given to Jesus Christ. We say that collect
for the Holy Souls, *Fidelium Deus omnium*, and think
we are asking God to have mercy on the souls of his
servants and hand-maids. But what we are really
asking him to do is to have mercy on the souls of his
men and women slaves. The lash, the branding-iron,
crucifixion—those were the punishments which the
lord could deal out to his slaves at the time when the
Bible was written. And it is that kind of atmosphere
which we have somehow to recover before we can
realize, even remotely, what is meant when we say
we believe Jesus Christ is our Lord.

The point is that he owns us. We are always forgetting that, simply because he is so good to us; but
the plain fact is that he redeemed us, that is to say,
he bought us, and we belong to him. You and I have
never seen a slave. It was a common enough sight a
hundred and fifty years ago, but now, thank God,
there are very few left in the world; how, then, are
you and I to imagine what it means, *belonging* to Jesus
Christ? One human being doesn't, nowadays, belong
to another. I suppose our Lord saw that coming, and
took it into account. And that is, perhaps, why he
made things easier for us by encouraging us to think

of ourselves, in relation to him, not as human beings, but as animals. " We are his people," the psalm says, " and the sheep of his pasture." Our Lord took up the echoes of that old psalm, and told us, " I am the good Shepherd ".

We belong to our Lord, that is, our Owner, just as the farmer's sheep belong to the farmer; that is why we carry his mark. If you have had anything to do with sheep, you will know that they have an incorrigible habit of squirming their way through hedges and getting mixed up with the sheep of the farmer next door. And that is why, especially when sheep are turned out to graze on hill-sides, the farmer who owns them puts a sort of splotch on their sides, rather like what happened to you the last time you spilt the red ink. And so, if they do get straying and mix up with other people's flocks, there's no great harm done. So it was that, when you were baptized, our Lord put his mark on you, the sign of the cross. You and I can't see it there, because it belongs to the supernatural, not to the natural order; but an angel can see whether you are baptized or not, just as easily as you or I can see when somebody's got a smut on their nose. And that mark is indelible; it never comes out. Not that our Lord would find any difficulty in recognizing us without a mark to distinguish us. He calls his own sheep by name, the Gospel tells us; when you are christened you are given a set of names; and by those names he thinks of you, My sheep So-and-so. To us, of course, one sheep looks exactly like another. But Mr. Vaughan could tell you which was which among a lot of the sheep here, and where each of them came from; although he doesn't call them by name,

except the cade lamb up at the Hurst, which is
called Sam. A shepherd who has a whole-time job
looking after sheep comes to know pretty well all of
them apart. And the good Shepherd knows you and
me individually, knows all the millions of Christians
in the world by their Christian names.

One bother about sheep getting through hedges is
that they are apt to come across food which doesn't
agree with them. If a sheep gets loose in clover, for
example, I'm sorry to say that it eats too much of it;
and when that happens it swells out to an enormous
size and lies down on its side and can't get up. It's all
very well laughing, but if you will examine your own
conscience you will find it difficult not to have a kind
of sneaking sympathy with the sheep's point of view.
That's why our Lord says he leads his sheep out and
finds them pasture; he arranges that they shall feed
on what is good for them. And that is where I come
in; that is where the clergy come in. The shepherd
doesn't run after the sheep when they get straying;
he shouts to his dog, and the dog runs after them,
barking at them in a very rude way. When you see a
sheep-dog doing that, it ought to remind you of my
sermons; you should think of the clergy yapping at
you and saying, " You ought to do this ", and " You
mustn't do that "; they do it because they are acting
under the Shepherd's orders. I don't say the clergy
don't sometimes enjoy it; but then, I dare say the
sheep-dog enjoys it. The point is that the clergy,
like sheep-dogs, aren't just making up rules for you;
they are telling you what the Shepherd wants you to
do, the Shepherd who owns you.

Sheep can't live out in a field and eat grass all the

year round. At least they can, but they wouldn't thrive on it; the farmer has to give them swedes and things; and sheep, you must remember, don't share our great dislike of vegetables. You and I couldn't live our supernatural lives properly if the good Shepherd didn't give us supernatural food; and what that is you all know—he gives us his own Body and Blood in the Holy Eucharist. But we haven't time to stop and think about that now.

And then there's one last picture our Lord has given us, the most familiar of all; the good Shepherd going out in search of the lost sheep. He owns us, and he can't bear to lose us. We are all familiar with the picture, but there's one thing we tend to forget about it. When a sheep gets caught, say, in a bush, and the shepherd comes to free it, you don't find the sheep sitting there quiet under the process; it struggles like mad—to get away from the shepherd. He has to save it in spite of itself. And so it is with a human soul that has fallen into grave sin; the grace which sets it free is something it doesn't want, something it is tempted to refuse. Somebody ought to paint a picture of the good Shepherd coming to rescue his sheep, and the sheep trying to get away.

One question ought to have been occurring to you all this time, if you were more intelligent than you are. You ought to be wondering, "If we call our Lord by that name because he owns us, on what principle do we call the Blessed Virgin our Lady? Does she, too, own us?" I don't think it's quite the same idea; but our time has run out now, and we will have to talk about our Lady next Sunday instead.

VIII

Conceived by the Holy Ghost, born of the Virgin Mary

THERE is a father of the Church called St. Tarasius,
and I'm sorry to say that I know nothing whatever
about him, except that an extremely long and rather
trying passage from one of his sermons came into the
office yesterday, the Saturday in the Octave of the
Immaculate Conception. He addresses our Lady in
a series of very elaborate titles, mostly taken from the
Old Testament; and among other things he says,
" Hail, thou light cloud, that dost scatter the heavenly
rain ". At first, you rather wonder what he is talking
about; but if you know your Bible very well, which
I'm afraid most of us don't, you will remember that
the prophet Isaias once said, " Behold, the Lord shall
go up on a light cloud, and shall enter into Egypt ".
Well, that begins to put the thing more in its proper
setting, and it's rather a nice idea, really, to think of
the Flight into Egypt in that way—St. Joseph trudging
along, on those hard winter roads, and our Lady
jogging along on the donkey's back, which isn't a
really comfortable way of going long distances, though
it's all right just for a few hundred yards at Folkestone,
on the soft sand. But our Lord, you see, rests quietly
on our Lady's breast, borne along as if on a light
cloud.

And you can think of it in another way; you can
think of a country all parched with drought, and the

63

farmers all scratching their heads and tapping the barometer and hoping for a nice drop of rain because what'll happen to the roots otherwise, and then a light cloud rising in the monotonous calm of the sky, with the promise of rain at last. That's how the world was, you see, when our Lord came, parched, dry, waiting for its redemption. And the cloud which brought promise of rain was the appearance on earth of our Blessed Lady, ready to bring down from heaven the precious Dew of Grace which would bring life into our starved natures once more.

But there's another thing about clouds, since we have started talking about them. They look different when you catch them in different lights, from different angles. When you are in a cloud, it's just a sort of dank mist all round you. When you look up at it from below, it may be a nice fluffy white thing, like a piece of cotton wool hanging in the air. Or again, it may be a dark, threatening presence in the sky, like an enormous blot on your letter home. Or it may catch the colours of sunset, and be all red and gold wreathing itself into strange shapes that make you think of a golden stair-way or a harbour jutting out into calm seas. But it's all the same cloud, really. And so it is that the figure of our Blessed Lady presents itself in different ways to the minds of men in different ages, according to the special needs of one age or another.

I was saying to you at the end of my sermon last Sunday that I didn't think we use the words " our Lady " quite in the same way as we use the words " our Lord ". When we call Jesus Christ our Lord, we mean that he owns us, because that title comes down to us from an age when you thought of a " lord " as a man who owned slaves. But the title " our Lady " doesn't come down to us from very far back in history. I may be wrong, but I think you could read all through the Missal and the Breviary without finding the Blessed Virgin referred to as " our Lady " once. That title, I think, comes down to us from the Middle Ages, from the days of the troubadours; in those days, you talked about " your lady " meaning the woman you were in love with. In the very early days of the Church, you thought of the Blessed Virgin as the Mother of God, because that was what the heretics wouldn't see. In the Middle Ages, you thought of her as our Lady, because the whole notion of man's love for woman was being refined into something purer and nobler than it had been hitherto. After the Reformation, when kings and queens became much more important in the world, you thought of the Blessed Virgin as the Queen of Heaven. And today, when family life is so important, and people have begun to take more notice of children, we are apt to think of her more simply as the Mother of the Infant Jesus.

All that I dare say you find rather boring. Well, this afternoon, discussing these two clauses in the *Credo*, " Conceived by the Holy Ghost, born of the Virgin Mary ", we've got to think of our Lady not under any fancy title, but in terms of plain fact. Our Lord was born—that is to say, our Lady was really his Mother; his body was really built up from hers, just like the body of any other human being. His body wasn't a phantom, wasn't a special creation; it grew, before and after birth, as human bodies grow. So we do well to think of our Lady as the patroness of motherhood. But at the same time, our Lady is a Virgin, and the patron of Virginity. When we pronounce the words " Blessed Mary ever-Virgin "— we usually try to pronounce them as one syllable—we are saying three separate things. The first is, that our Lady was still a Virgin when our Lord was conceived. She had not, like all other women who have achieved the dignity of motherhood, given herself to a man; our Lord had no father. The second is, that she was a Virgin when our Lord was born. Her child-bearing cost her none of that pain which child-bearing costs other women, and left, in her, no traces of its happening. And the third is—what we should expect—that she remained a Virgin the rest of her life.

Now, remember—all this seems quite obvious to you and me. I don't say it seems quite natural, because clearly it isn't natural; but it seems quite obvious. Granted that our Lord was what he was, we should expect him to come into the world in some supernatural way. If you are given a concertina by your father for a Christmas present, you like it to be all wrapped up in shiny paper with robins on it, and tied with gold string. I don't say that that will happen this year, because the paper controller may not want to release enough paper to wrap up a concertina in, if it's a good large concertina, to rouse the echoes of the dormitory with; and for all I know the string controller will say there's no more gold string left, because it's all been used to pack land-mines. But that's the idea of the thing, that's what you expect. If your father is going to give you something really splendid and really expensive, you don't expect him to take it out of a drawer and throw it across the room at you and say, " Hi, here's a concertina "; the thing has got to be done properly. And so it is, if we may compare very big things with very little things, in this matter of our Lord's birth. God was giving us the most splendid present, the most expensive present, that anybody has ever given anybody. And you would *expect* that this present of his should be wrapped up in an air of supernatural mystery; that angels should come wandering into poor folks' houses at Nazareth, and odd things going on up in the sky should worry the astronomers in Chaldaea. It all seems so obvious; surely anybody could understand *that* bit of the *Credo*, unless he didn't believe in miracles at all.

But you know, it's not quite so simple. You may find yourself arguing with somebody who isn't a Catholic, isn't even much of a Christian, but is prepared to regard miracles as possible; and still you may find that he doesn't want to believe in this miracle of the Virgin Birth. He will say something like this: " The Resurrection, yes, I understand that. And I can see that if it is possible for a man to rise again when he has been three days in the tomb, it is possible for a man to be born without a father. But I don't quite see why anybody should have *wanted* the Virgin Birth to happen. After all, you make a great point of it that in the Incarnation God really became man; it wasn't just a phantom or an apparition, it was a real man of flesh and blood who was, all the time, Almighty God. Surely we should have felt much more certain of that if he had been born just like anybody else, if he had had a father as well as a mother? And you

Catholics are always telling us that marriage is a high and holy vocation, that there's nothing wrong about sex, sin only comes in when sex is used as it wasn't meant to be used; surely we should have felt much more certain of that if the Blessed Virgin had been really married to St. Joseph, and they had had a family just like other people?" When it's put like that, the difficulty isn't quite so easy to answer.

I think the right answer is this. The Resurrection, through which our Lord passed out of his mortal life, is meant to assure us that life is a bigger thing than death. The Virgin Birth, by which he entered into his mortal life, is meant to assure us that spirit is a bigger thing than body. Let me just explain what I mean.

Adam and Eve, when they were in Paradise, had bodies and souls tied together just as yours and mine are, just as mysteriously as yours and mine are. But, with them, the soul was always and obviously the leading partner in that companionship. The soul gave orders, and the body obeyed them. I even read a book the other day—not by a Catholic, but by a very intelligent man—which suggested that, before the Fall, man's will directed his digestion. Think how nice it would be if you could digest your meals at will, like brushing your teeth. And if Mother Clare, on a bright summer day, said, " You can't go and bathe yet, because you haven't digested your lunch ", you would say, " All right, Mother, give me two minutes, and I'll do that now ". Instead of that, we have to wait for our lunch to digest itself; and sometimes we get indigestion, and you will find that with older people, sometimes even with schoolmasters and schoolmistresses, indigestion puts them in a bad temper. Indigestion puts them in a bad temper—do you see what has happened? Indigestion, which is a matter concerned with the body, has given rise to bad temper, which is a matter concerned with the soul. The body, which ought to be taking its orders from the soul, is giving its orders to the soul instead! That is the kind of thing the Fall has let us in for. It puts the cart before the horse. If you can imagine Princess, harnessed the wrong way round in a pony-cart, so as to face it, being pulled by the pony-cart down a very steep hill—that is the sort of thing that is happening to us all the time since the Fall. I don't mean that the body *always* gets the better of us. But we can never be sure when it *will* get the better of us, and we can never be sure, from moment to moment, whether it *isn't* getting the better of us. It's got an unfair pull, and it's always trying to run away with us, wanting to eat too much, wanting to lie in bed too long, and so on. We always find ourselves thinking, " Now, was that really all right; that last éclair, that last five minutes? Or did my body take command of the situation when my soul kind of wasn't looking? " We are never quite certain of ourselves, are we?

And that complicates, enormously, our feelings about love and marriage. The love of man and woman is, perhaps, the highest and noblest thing there is in the natural order. And yet, where marriage is concerned, the body comes in so much that we're always afraid of this high and noble thing degenerating into mere passion. Don't mistake me; the body's got to come in; marriage was instituted before the Fall, not after it. But, since the Fall, as I say, we are uneasy about the body; we are always afraid of its trying to get the upper hand. So many people go wrong over this business of sex, wreck their peace of mind over it and, we fear, lose their souls over it, that the whole subject becomes embittered for us. It humiliates us to see the human race so often at the mercy of its passions; the body so often tyrannizing over the immortal soul. And sometimes we are almost tempted to throw up the whole thing, to admit, in spite of our better judgement, that matter is superior to mind, that our bodies are the things we ought to live for, not our souls.

And then Christmas comes round, and with Christmas the memory of the Virgin Birth, and we know it's all right. Just as Easter tells us we were fools to doubt life is stronger than death, so Christmas tells us we were fools to doubt that the soul, not the body, is the nobler part. " Conceived by the Holy Ghost, born of the Virgin Mary "—spirit first, then matter. St. Leo, in a passage we read in the divine office on Christmas Day, has a fine phrase: " she who was to be entrusted with this sacred charge was to conceive in the mind first, and only afterwards in the body." You see, it is as if the message brought by Gabriel first imprinted on her thoughts the image of the Saviour who was to come, and thereupon the reality of that image began to form itself in her womb. The doubters, the defeatists were wrong: the Word was made flesh in order that we, creatures of flesh, might be brought, once more, under the power of the Spirit.

IX

He suffered

I EXPECT some of you will be wanting to complain
that I've only given you half a clause out of the *Credo*
there, instead of a whole clause. When you say the
Credo, you say, " Sufton Pontius Pilate ", and that's
that. But, you see, quite apart from the question *when*
or *how* our Lord suffered, it is important to get it into
our heads that he *did* suffer. Go back for a moment to
what you remember of the Gospels, and tell me what
evidence we have, earlier than his agony in the garden
of Gethsemani, to tell us that our Lord *did* suffer? It's
not so easy, is it? I think I'm right in saying that there
are only three occasions, before Gethsemani, on which
we hear of our Lord as suffering any kind of bodily
discomfort. When his temptation in the wilderness
was over, we are told that he hungered. When
he passed by the fig-tree that had leaves but no
fruit on it, we are told that he was hungry. And
when he sat down by the well and talked to the
woman of Samaria, we are told that he was tired
after his journey. Elsewhere we hear of his being
sorry about things—he wept over Jerusalem, for
example, and over the grave of Lazarus—but except
on those three occasions I don't think we ever hear
that he suffered bodily discomfort—till Gethsemani.

So, you see, it isn't necessary to explain away a
great deal, if you want to persuade yourself that our

Lord never experienced human suffering. There were heretics in early days, as I think I told you before, who thought that; who made out that our Lord didn't really become a man at his Incarnation; he only wore a kind of phantom body, something like a ghost. And in our own day the Christian Scientists —the people who tell you that you haven't really got a tooth-ache, you've only got a stupid idea that you've got a tooth-ache, and therefore the best thing to do is to pray about it, instead of going to the dentist—the Christian Scientists would tell you that our Lord didn't suffer. Oh, no, he was perfectly wise, and therefore he knew that there was no such thing as suffering, and that is why he went about persuading the blind people that they weren't blind, and the lepers that they weren't lepers, and Lazarus that he wasn't dead. If you are perfectly holy, they say, then you must be perfectly healthy. And, you know, it's good Catholic theology, though I don't know whether it's a matter of faith, that our Lord while he was on earth never suffered from any *disease*. His human body was such a perfect thing that it couldn't go wrong of its own accord; it was only when he treated it roughly (or when other people treated it roughly) that it could enter into Adam's uncomfortable legacy of pain.

However, there it is; our Lord *was* hungry, *was* tired, *did* suffer, even before Pontius Pilate comes into the picture at all. And at the same time his whole life, as it is recorded for us in the Gospels, is a kind of campaign against suffering—no more blind, no more deaf, no more lame, no more paralytics, no more lepers, that seems to be his ideal. Now, you ask yourself, is suffering a good thing or a bad thing? If it is a good thing, why did he spend so much of his time in making it disappear from the countryside round him, when he might have been attending, instead, to the needs of people's souls? And if suffering is a bad thing, why did he make himself so uncomfortable, why did he choose such an uncomfortable life, why did he bring upon himself—for it is evident all through that he brought it on himself—a death attended by such crowded circumstances of pain? What are we to make of suffering ourselves? Is it a thing to run away from, or is it a thing we ought to welcome? *He* suffered; our Lord suffered; what about his servants?

Well, let us take the answer to that question bit by bit. In the first place, suffering is of its own nature a bad thing, not a good thing. When I say that it's a bad thing, I don't mean of course that it's *wicked* to have a tooth-ache; I don't want to have you coming round to me on Saturday evening and confessing that you've had a slight attack of neuralgia. I mean that suffering is an imperfection, brought into this world of ours by the fall of man: it's a blot on creation, it degrades us. And therefore, in the presence of a very good person, suffering tends to run away and hide itself; when our Lord met a leper, the leprosy couldn't maintain itself, it fled from his presence. And so it has been in the lives of his saints. You can read in the Bible how a dead man was being carried out to burial once, when a party of invading Syrians appeared; and the undertaker and his assistants thought it would be a good thing to cut short the funeral procession, so they dropped the corpse into the nearest tomb they could see. It happened to be the tomb of the prophet Eliseus, who had just died. And the dead man immediately came to life. Death, you may say, couldn't bear to find itself anywhere near anyone as holy as Eliseus, just as the undertaker couldn't bear to be near a party of invading Syrians. Death said (as it were), " Oh, gosh, I can't stand this ", and ran away, leaving the man to come to life. That's putting it rather crudely, but you see what I mean; suffering is of its own nature an evil, and it tends to disappear when it is brought into contact with a very holy person, just as darkness disappears when you bring a candle into a room.

Well then, if suffering is an evil, that means that you and I have got a right to avoid it. If you've got a tooth-ache, you've a perfect right to have the tooth taken out, instead of saying, " No, thanks, I'd rather offer it up ". And indeed it means that you have a *duty* of looking after your health, because your health is one of God's good gifts, and it isn't polite of you to throw it away carelessly as if you attached no value to it; any more than it would be polite if your rich uncle gives you half a crown to throw it out of the window and say you can get on very well without it. If suffering is an evil, that means that you must not inflict it on other people. I remember a small boy— only he isn't a small boy now, he's grown into rather a great man—who was teasing his sister, and when she complained of this treatment he replied, " A slight mortification, my dear, can only help to get you off Purgatory." That won't do; suffering is an evil, and human beings mustn't inflict it on one another, unless it is for the sake of securing a greater good—as, for instance, when the dentist inflicts suffering on you because that is the only way of stopping a bad tooth.

And again, if suffering is an evil, we must do our best to relieve the sufferings of other people. We must feed the hungry and look after the sick; or if we can't do it ourselves we must contribute to the charities that do. All these centuries Christianity has been preaching that suffering isn't what really matters, sin is what really matters. And yet, all these centuries, Christianity has been founding hospitals and running soup-kitchens, because it knows that suffering is, in itself, an evil. I suppose that was part of the reason why our Lord, in Gethsemani, prayed to be delivered from the chalice of his Passion. He wanted to show us that suffering is an evil, and unless it is clearly God's will that it should come to us, we have a right to try and avoid it.

But sometimes, you see, it is God's will that suffering should come to us, and that we should *not* be able to avoid it. How is that? Well, we tried to go into all that last term, when we were talking about the Fall, and how suffering was the appropriate punishment of sin. The whole human race has sinned, and the whole human race has got to suffer; the bit of suffering which comes your way and mine is just you and me doing our bit. We have said that suffering is an evil thing in itself. But the suffering which comes to us in this way, suffering which we can't avoid because it is God's will for us, can be turned from an evil thing into a good thing, *if* we treat it in the right way. If you look at an electric light bulb when it isn't burning, you will see nothing inside but a rather uninteresting-looking bit of wire; and you might be tempted to say to yourself, " I don't see how anybody's going to get light out of that." But, once you switch the current on, that piece of wire does give light, because the electricity transmutes it into a glowing mass. So it is with suffering in human lives; an evil thing in itself, it becomes a good thing when it is transmuted, by the love of God, into a glowing focus of charity.

Let's be a little more practical. We turn this evil thing, suffering, into a good thing when we accept it as God's will for us. I've tried to explain to you already that the only way in which we human beings can justify our existence in creation at all is to obey God's will for us. That is what we are FOR. A human being who is not out to obey God's will is exactly as much use in his creation as a tooth-brush is in the possession of a man who has had all his teeth taken out. And there are two ways in which we can obey God's will, by *doing* what he wants us to do, and by *suffering* what he wants us to suffer. There's this trouble about *doing* what God wants us to do—that it's so often, at the same time, the thing *we* want to do. Even if it is the kind of thing that doesn't sound very attractive at the first go-off, even if it means (say) going out and being a missionary in foreign parts, or washing dishes all day in a canteen, it's extraordinary how people get to like it, and take a pride in doing it well, and want to go on doing it. That means that we are never quite sure whether we are doing what is God's will because it is God's will, or because it is ours. Self-love, self-admiration, will go on creeping in and disturbing the purity of our motives. But with suffering it's different; I mean, when it's suffering God sends us, suffering we can't get out of. It's almost impossible to feel any pride about that; almost impossible to get any kick, as we say, out of that. And if God calls on you to spend twenty years lying on your back, in pain most of the time, and you go on telling him that it is his will, and you want it to happen because it is his will, then, believe me, you are in a fair way to going straight to heaven.

There is another way in which you and I can turn this evil thing, suffering, into something good; and that is by uniting it with the sufferings of Jesus Christ. We saw that, when he made atonement for our sins, he made it in full. He was perfectly sinless, and therefore it was his right, if he had wished it, to live without suffering; it is only because we are all sinners that we have all got to be sufferers. But he, of his own will, took our punishment upon himself; he would be hungry, and thirsty, and tired out, on the roads of Galilee; and at the end of his life he would go through a long pageant of suffering, which ended with death on a Cross. And all the saints have realized that their job was to suffer in union with Christ. St. Paul even talks of himself as paying off " that which is lacking of the sufferings of Christ ". He thinks of our Lord as a rich Benefactor who has paid off, once for all, the debt of suffering we owed, and now it is for us to pay back that debt to him, as far as we can, by enduring our own sufferings in union with him. So it is that you get this same curious contradiction about the saints' lives which you find in our Lord's own life; they are always relieving the sufferings of other people, and at the same time welcoming suffering for themselves. You've all heard of Bernadette Soubirous, who had the visions of our Lady at Lourdes, and scratched up with her own hands the spring of water which has brought health, since then, to so many thousands of people. She became a nun, and it was found, before long, that she was suffering from a very painful and an incurable disease. But there was one moment at which she seemed a little better, and even fit to travel; so the Reverend Mother of her convent came to her and said they had arranged a nice treat for her. She was to go back to Lourdes as a pilgrim, and ask the beautiful Lady of her visions if she might not be cured among the rest—surely there could be no doubt that HER prayer would be listened to! But Bernadette immediately said, " No; the spring is not for me." The spring is not for me; it was her business, as a saint, to win healing for other people; it was her business as a saint to win, not healing, but suffering, for herself.

One further question obviously occurs to one's mind. If we ought to welcome the suffering which God sends us whether we like it or not, oughtn't we, perhaps, to be taking on extra mortifications on our own, deliberately making ourselves uncomfortable, so as to have *more* suffering to unite with his? Well, of course, the saints have always done that, scourging themselves and wearing hair-shirts and so on. And there *are* very good people who do that sort of thing, but I don't think it is to be encouraged for the ordinary run of Christians. It *can* make you proud, it *can* make you self-righteous, it *can* make you unsympathetic to other people. When I say that, I'm not referring of course to self-denial. Giving up sweets in Lent, I mean, is perfectly all right, as long as the doctor assures you that sweets are not absolutely necessary to your health. But I don't think we ought to spend our time trying to think up ways of positively making ourselves uncomfortable, by putting salt instead of sugar in our tea and so on. We ought to ask God to make us very holy people; and perhaps when he has done that he will let us know what greater sacrifices he wants us to make for him, under our confessor's advice. Meanwhile, it's best for us to stick to ordinary ways, and content ourselves with bearing, for his sake, the mortifications which come to us from his hands.

X

Under Pontius Pilate

THERE are only two human beings—merely human beings—who are referred to by name, whether in the Apostles' Creed or in the Nicene Creed which is said at Mass. One is our Blessed Lady, and that is natural enough. She is the touch-stone of Christian truth. I bet you don't know what a touch-stone is, though it's a word you are always coming across in books; I didn't myself till I looked it up just now in the dictionary. If you want to test the amount of gold or silver there is in something made of alloyed metal, a wristwatch it may be, or a half-crown, you get hold of a particular kind of stone, which is dark black, and you scratch your piece of metal along it—probably it makes a very unpleasant squeak, but that can't be helped—and you can tell by the colour of the scratch it makes whether your piece of metal was pure gold, pure silver, or how much it was alloyed with other metals. And when I call our Lady the touch-stone of Christian truth, I mean this—that if you remember to call our Blessed Lady the Mother of God, you won't be likely to fall into any error about the doctrine of the Incarnation. And if you meet somebody whom you suspect of holding queer views about the Incarnation, the best thing is to say, " Of course, you do admit that the Blessed Virgin Mary was the Mother

of God, don't you? " And if they hum and haw about
it, you know that their ideas of the Incarnation are
not good, hundred per cent Catholic doctrine; your
touch-stone has found them out.

But when it comes to Pontius Pilate, poor Pilate
wasn't the touch-stone of anything; certainly not of
truth—he didn't even believe in truth. I call him poor
Pilate, because that is the way he always strikes me in
the Gospel story. I know you see pictures of him, in
the Stations of the Cross, for example, which seem
to represent him as a very wicked man; but I can
never think of him except as a hopelessly weak man,
a fuffler and a shuffler who never ought to have got his
job as procurator at all. The trouble about him, I
suppose, was that he was so anxious to please everybody. He wanted to please Caiphas, he wanted to
please the Jewish mob, he wanted to please his wife,
he wanted to please Herod, he wanted to please our
Lord, he wanted to please St. Joseph of Arimathea;
and, like most people who want to please everybody,
he pleased nobody. The Jews, when he resigned his
office, followed him to Rome and had him condemned for managing his province so badly; so he got
nothing out of *them*. And meanwhile, we Christians
have pilloried him in the *Credo*, and all over the world
Pilate will be remembered, to the end of time, as the
man who missed his chance. You can see him,
can't you, washing his hands; I expect he was always
washing his hands, like one of those oily shopkeepers
who come up to you and say, " What can I have the
pleasure of doing for you to-day, madam? " At Mount
Pilatus, in Switzerland, they have a legend that Pilate's
body lies in a lake near the top of the mountain; and

every now and again he comes out and is seen by
wanderers on the mountain side, always washing his
hands.

"What is truth?" Pilate asked, and it serves him
right that he should be put there in the middle of the
Credo, as if the Church were determined to go on
saying to him, to the end of time, "Here, you fool,
this is!" But why is it the man who was so weak,
not the men who were so wicked? Why Pilate, not
Judas, not Caiphas? Well, I think you can give
pretty good reasons for that. In the first place, putting
Pilate's name in the middle of the document which
we flourish in people's faces when they think they want
to join the Church, has the effect of *anchoring down*
the Christian religion to a definite point in history.
Jesus Christ is not an imaginary person, like Jupiter,
or Odin, or Osiris; when you tell his story, you don't
have to begin, like the fairy stories, with the words,
"Once on a time". No, you can say quite definitely,
"Jesus Christ was a carpenter, who lived in Palestine,
roughly at the 33rd degree of latitude and the 35th
degree of longitude, in the reign of the emperor
Tiberius, under the local administration of Pontius
Pilate, rather more than 1,900 years ago". God, in
becoming incarnate, condescended to our level; the
Divine Word, who is altogether outside time, consented to be born in the year 753 after the foundation
of Rome, or thereabouts, and to become dependent,
while he was on earth, on the lapse of time, days and
years and minutes. It is this *pegging down* of the
Christian revelation to a particular moment in history,
and a particular background or context of history, that
the Church insists upon when she tells us to say,

morning after morning, " I believe that he was
crucified under Pontius Pilate ". Catholic scholars
are not agreed about the exact date of our Lord's birth.
Probably the old dating was wrong, and he was born
in the year which we call 4 B.C., or perhaps even earlier
than that, perhaps as early as the year we call 8 B.C.
They are at full liberty to differ with one another, and
to hold the views they prefer about that. But the date
of our Lord's death is fixed for them within a ten years'
limit; it must have happened between the year A.D.
26 and the year A.D. 36, because those were the first
and last years of Pilate's administration. If you say
that he died before 26, or after 36, then you are not
just saying something which is offensive to pious ears,
or temerarious, or contrary to the tradition of the
Church; you are saying something which is *heresy*.
For the dates are in the Creed, and it is heresy to contradict the Creed.

And if people say, " Why did God choose that
particular moment of history, rather than some other
moment in history? " your answer can still be,
" Pontius Pilate ". The governorship of Pontius Pilate
fills ten years within those hundred years of history
which were most appropriate, in the whole annals of
the human race, for the Incarnation to happen in.
About three hundred years before our Lord was born,
King Alexander of Macedon, who already ruled the
whole of Greece, set out to conquer Asia. By the
time he died—and he died young—he was ruling over
the whole of the Near East, Turkey, Iran, Iraq and
Egypt, and, incidentally, Palestine. His empire broke
up after he was dead, but what it meant was this, that
all the Eastern part of the civilized world had a

common language; it could all talk Greek. Not
frightfully good Greek, no doubt; I suppose in many
places it was rather like your French; but still, it was
possible to make yourself understood in Greek all
over the part of the world which we now call the Near
East; and that, you can see for yourselves, was a great
advantage if a revelation was going to be brought
from heaven which was meant for the whole of mankind.

And then, during the hundred and fifty years or so
before our Lord came, the Roman Empire took control. Mummius conquered Greece and Scipio
conquered Carthage and Pompey conquered Spain
and Caesar conquered Gaul, and one way and another
the whole of the Mediterranean world, from Portugal
to Persia, looked like Mussolini's dream—it was all
one Roman Empire. That meant peace and trade
and a network of admirable roads; it meant that the
world was kept in order by Roman officials everywhere, some of them time-servers like Pontius Pilate
but not, on the whole, a weak lot of men. For all
intents and purposes, when our Lord came, there
was a single world-empire, the Roman Empire, there
was a single world-language, the Greek language.
That had never happened before; it has never happened since. Our Lord came just at the right time; or
rather, if you look at it from a more sensible point of
view, Providence had arranged the right time for our
Lord to come in. Up till 30 B.C., he would have found
the world distracted by a long series of civil wars. After
A.D. 70 he would have found Jerusalem a heap of ruins.
Just in those hundred years, everything was favourable, you see, to the spread of a world-wide Gospel.

Well, that's enough history. Is there any other kind of theological importance we can attach to the words, " He suffered under Pontius Pilate "? Why yes, I think there is. I think we are also meant to reflect, when we say that clause in the *Credo*, that the Christian religion always has one enemy, and always it is the same enemy, the world. Of course, you can talk about " the world " in several different senses. It can mean the habitable globe on which we live, revolving round the sun and, in shape, an oblate spheroid. When we used to ask, at school, what an oblate spheroid was like, they used to say, " Oh, like an orange ". Now that none of you ever sees an orange, I don't know what they tell you. Never mind, we are not going to talk about the world in that sense. Or you may mean by the world the total number of human beings, white, black and yellow, good, bad or indifferent, who contrive to live in the world. That's not what I mean by the world, when I say that the world is the enemy of the Christian religion.

What do we mean when we talk about " worldly " people? It isn't a very easy thing to explain or to define. But, roughly speaking, I think you can say worldly people are the people who either don't believe in a future life, or don't bother about a future life, and want to make this world as comfortable a place as possible for as many people as possible, always including themselves. They want everything to be efficiently run, trains going as punctually as possible, and food and drink and cinemas as cheap as possible, and newspapers as large and as chatty as possible, and nothing to make any disturbance in people's lives— " Live and let live " is their motto. And of course all

that was what Pontius Pilate stood for. He didn't care
a bit about whether our Lord was the Son of God or
not, about whether he broke the sabbath or not, about
whether he kept the law of Moses or not. He only
wanted to keep the Jews reasonably contented, reasonably quiet; he didn't want crowds of people going
round shouting out slogans like " Hosanna to the Son
of David ", or " Crucify him "—that kind of thing
was bad for public safety, so it had got to be stopped.
It wasn't Judas, you see, it wasn't Caiphas, that
crucified our Lord. If they had done it, there was an
intelligible motive for doing it. Caiphas and those
others had at least the excuse of wounded professional
pride, for wanting to put our Lord to death. Judas
had a much more practical excuse—thirty pieces of
silver. But Pilate didn't dislike our Lord at all; he was
rather impressed by him, he was certainly convinced
of his innocence. And yet it was Pilate who crucified
him. It was the world of worldly people, with its
dislike of a scene, its dislike of a fuss, its doctrine of
" Live and let live " that put Jesus Christ to death.

I don't mean, of course, to suggest that our Lord
disobeyed the civil authorities of his time, and was
put to death for that. Often you will find stupid people
talking as if our Lord had been a political agitator of
some sort, and speculating whether, if he came back
to the world nowadays, he wouldn't be a Communist.
Nothing could be more untrue to history than talking
like that. Our Lord called the scribes and Pharisees
hypocrites, he called King Herod " that fox "; but we
are never told that he said anything impolite about the
Roman authorities. When people tried to get him
interested in the story of how Pilate had massacred a

lot of Galileans, his own fellow-countrymen, he deliberately changed the subject. And when they asked him about paying tribute, he said, " Render to Caesar the things that are Caesar's ". That's one of the most curious things about our Lord; he came and lived in Palestine at a time when I suppose the Romans were about as unpopular as a foreign invader could be and he didn't stir a finger against them. It wasn't for him to mix himself up in political quarrels, and it is not for his Church to do that either.

No, the reason why Pilate consented to crucify our Lord was because the whole of our Lord's teaching was a challenge to the worldly people who found the world a comfortable place, and wanted to go on being comfortable, and not thinking about God or heaven or hell. And that is really why the Christian Church is always being persecuted, century after century, in this part of the world or that. She will not let people alone, she will go on reminding them of uncomfortable things. You know what it's like if seven people are sitting in a railway-carriage on a rather cold day, with both windows up and all the heating on and a really good fug to sit in; and then at some way-side station an eighth traveller gets in who opens the window to look out and say good-bye to his wife and then doesn't quite pull it up to the top, so that some of the cold air gets in. That is how the world feels about the Christian Church, with her talk of heaven and hell. And all that, remember, affects you and me. Because there is always the temptation, for you and me, to lie rather low about being Christians, out of human respect, when we are living among people who don't share our beliefs; to talk as if sin didn't matter very much, and God didn't mind very much, and there was no heaven or hell to worry about. But, although there is no sense in trying to ram our beliefs down people's throats all the time, that temptation I have been speaking of is one we have got to be on our guard against. When we say the *Credo*, and find ourselves repeating the words, " He suffered under Pontius Pilate ", we have got to remind ourselves that it is not our business, as Christians, to toady and flatter Pontius Pilate, that is, the world.

I think I have heard a story of a small boy who was asked to recite the Apostles' Creed and, after a good deal of humming and hawing and shifting from one leg to the other, said at last, " Please, teacher, I believe in Pontius Pilate ". That answer doesn't get full marks. But all the same we mustn't forget about Pontius Pilate when we say the Creed.

XI

Was crucified

CENTURIES ago two men were doing a job of work. I
suppose I oughtn't really to be talking to you about
work, when it's half-term; but then, these men
weren't working with their brains, they were working
with their hands, which (as we all know) is much
pleasanter. They had just felled a tree, not a very
tall one; and they lopped off all the branches at the
top, and left them lying about to get in everybody's
way, as we all do; and then they cut a notch at one end
of the trunk, and drove a wedge into it, and hammered
and hammered at the wedge, until the trunk split in
two, and they were left with two rough stakes, round
on one side and flat on the other. Then they started
hacking away at the rounded side, chipping big pieces
off; and the younger man said, " What are we doing
this for? " and the elder man said, " Light enough for
a man to carry, and strong enough to carry a man;
that's the rule for doing this sort of work ". After
a time they'd just got two planks, more or less smooth
on both sides; but one of them was shorter than the
other because (I forgot to say) they had chopped off
nearly half of it. And when the younger man asked
why they chopped it off, the elder man said, " Light
enough for a man to carry, and strong enough to carry
a man; that's the rule for doing this sort of work ".

Then they laid down the shorter piece across the longer piece, not in the middle but close to one of its ends. And they got a couple of nails, and drove them through, so as to fasten the two planks together; and they wound some thick cord round the place where the two planks joined, and drew it tight and tied it up, so as to make the join stronger. And after that they stood back, and spat on their hands, and had a look at the job they'd been doing, just to see it was all right.

And the younger man said, " Seems to me as if we hadn't got it exactly true; the right arm seems to point up a bit, and the left arm down a bit ". And the older man said, " This isn't fancy work; as long as those nails hold, nobody is going to find any fault with you and me. Nothing's going to make a cross comfortable, and the man that's on it won't be too particular. Besides, you can't have everything; that's the third we've knocked together in two days ". " What beats me," said the younger man, " is why they want to execute them in such a clumsy way anyhow? Why can't they just strangle them, or club them to death? " " That shows you don't know what you're talking about," said the older man. " The point is, you've got to make an example of your criminal if you're going to impress these beastly provincials." (Did I mention that the two people we are concerned with were Roman soldiers? At least, they weren't exactly Roman; they were born somewhere in Bulgaria, but they were both in the Roman army, and wherever they went they always referred to the inhabitants of the country as " these beastly provincials ".) " There's been a lot of highway robbery going on lately, and nothing's going to stop it except the sight of a couple of robbers dying a very uncomfortable death just outside the city gates, where everyone passes. That's why we've got to make crosses for them." " And what about the man who was condemned this morning?" asked the other. " Was he a robber too?" " Why, no; you hear different accounts about him. Some say he tried to make himself King of the Jews; and other people will tell you that he was a harmless sort of man, who went about curing people when they were ill." " Oh, I see. And so he's got to be crucified so as to warn everybody else not to go about curing people when they're ill. . . . But does it really do very much good? A few years ago you couldn't take a country walk in Galilee without seeing crosses everywhere, just after the revolt; and now they say there's more trouble brewing, just the same kind as the last." " It's a fact," said the older man, " it doesn't do as much good as it ought. People have such short memories. There's been a lot of excitement and shouting about the man who was condemned this morning. And yet, I suppose, in a year's time everybody will have forgotten that he ever existed."

" Father, forgive them; they know not what they do." What would those two men have said, if you'd told them that the cross they had just knocked together out of two planks would be dug up, three hundred years later, and that in honour of that event the punishment of crucifixion would be abolished in the Roman Empire for ever? What would they have said, if you had told them that that cross would be taken away by the Parthians, and demanded back from the Parthians by one of the articles of a peace treaty?

That it would be carried into Jerusalem, in solemn procession, on the shoulders of the Emperor himself? That it would be broken up, as time went on, into little pieces, and those pieces would be treasured all over the world, in gold and silver reliquaries, exposed year by year for public adoration? That, all over the world, people would be worshipping in churches marked, inside and outside, with that cross; sacred ministers standing in front of that cross, attired in vestments marked, everywhere, with that cross, making the sign of that cross over a piece of bread marked with that cross? That school-boys and school-girls would see the figure of that cross in the rooms where they worked, or had their meals, or went to bed; that they would trace the lines of that cross, from forehead to breast, twenty or thirty times a day? All *that* was what those two men were doing when they knocked two pieces of wood together, that spring morning long ago. The instrument of punishment, used for slaves, so much held in contempt that men would say to one another, " Oh, go and crucify yourself! " when they were bored or angry, was to shine on the crowns of kings and emperors, was to be the symbol of a religion destined to pervade the world.

The cross is our symbol. Last Sunday I was talking to the devil, and the subject came up in our conversation. Many of you were present, but perhaps you weren't slick enough at your Latin to know who I was talking to—you may even have thought I was talking to you. I wasn't talking to you, I divided my remarks between the baby, and the devil, and the salt. And one of the things I said to the devil was,

Et hoc signum sanctae Crucis, quod nos fronti eius damus, tu maledicte diabole numquam audeas violare; which means, " And with this seal of holy Cross, which we here set on his forehead, accursed fiend, tamper thou never ". We concentrate the whole power of the Christian religion, the whole virtue of the Christian protest, in that single gesture. So that the cross is more than a symbol; it's a kind of talisman; it is part of the white magic which we Christians use in order to keep the devil as far away from us as possible. And when, in repeating the *Credo*, we say the words " was crucified ", we are not to think only of a historical fact, that Jesus Christ hung on a cross 1,900 years ago. We are to acknowledge our reverence for the cross itself as a sign of his empire. We salute it as our Union Jack, we proclaim its efficacy as a medicine against spiritual dangers. There were three things they tried to take away from us at the Reformation, I mean, three things chiefly, and we wouldn't part with any of them; our Lady, and the Mass, and the sign of the Cross.

You will meet stupid people, or read stupid books, or still more stupid articles in newspapers, which say the Cross isn't, originally, a Christian symbol; we took it over from the pagan religions that went before us. Now, as a matter of fact, it is quite extraordinary the way you *don't* find the cross in pagan religions. After all, what symbol could be easier to invent? Two lines intersecting one another at right-angles; you don't have to be terribly good at geometry to think of that. And what symbol could be more naturally expressive? Whenever you are going along a road, and another road cuts across it, you are confronted with the question, " Which way shall I take, this or this or this? " Of that hesitation, the cross is a natural image. And yet, if you look at a learned book which tells you about pre-Christian crosses and gives you pictures of them, all you will see is a tall pillar which has begun, in a very undecided way, to grow a sort of fungus at the top; it MIGHT be meant for a cross, but it looks rather more like an umbrella.

But, even if it were true that the cross was used as a symbol by the pagans, that would prove nothing. Because in any case they didn't use it with the same meaning as we do, for the same purpose as we do. An illiterate person, because he can't sign his name, makes a cross instead, and we call it " So-and-so, his mark." But when a bishop writes you a letter, he also puts a cross at the end of it; is that because he's illiterate and can't write his own surname? No, it's to show he's a bishop. What matters, you see, is not the cross itself but the reason for using it, the meaning we attach to it. And if the pagans used it, we have no notion what they meant by it, or what their reason was for using it. But our reason, our meaning, is perfectly clear. We draw pictures of the cross all over the place, we trace the lines of the cross over our own bodies, for one reason and for one reason only. We do it because two Roman soldiers, nineteen centuries ago, spent the first part of the morning hammering down one plank at right-angles to another.

It was a kind of glorious accident when they did that. Because they were providing us with a splendid symbol which we were going to use ever afterwards. There couldn't, you see, have been anything simpler. Imagine what a lot of fuss and bother it would mean if Hitler had decided, as he might easily have decided, that all Germans were to swastika themselves before and after every meal! Think what a tiresome business it would be trying to remember which way the tails of the swastika went, and with your soup getting cold the whole time! The cross—what could be simpler to draw? You draw the cross every time you do an addition sum. The cross—what could be a more familiar sight? Every time you look at the masts of a ship, or telegraph poles, or at a line of railings, you see the cross; it follows you everywhere.

And now, we have spoken of the cross as a symbol, which has a meaning; what exactly is its meaning? What exactly is it a symbol *of*? Well, there again, those two soldiers did much better than they knew. Because the cross hasn't just one meaning, it has hundreds. The other symbols mankind uses generally mean just one thing, and nothing more; the Rising Sun, for example, which is the symbol of Japan, or the Crescent which is the symbol of the Moham-medans—all those symbols mean just one thing, except the swastika, which means nothing whatever. But Christian thought goes on and on finding new meanings in the cross; it hasn't finished yet. It reminds us of all sorts of things in the Old Testament. The tree in Paradise, for example; the Preface for Passion-tide refers to the devil as having won his victory through a tree, and lost it through a tree. And Noe's Ark;—the Ark, covered all over with pitch, and the Cross, the Church points out to us, covered in the same way with our Lord's Precious Blood. And the brazen serpent which Moses lifted up on a pole in the wilderness, so that the people who had been bitten

by poisonous snakes could look at it and be healed—
our Lord himself compared his crucifixion to that.
And crucifixion itself, brutal and horrible punishment
as it was, does nevertheless suggest all sorts of gracious
images to the mind; we think of our Lord as lifted up
from the earth, looking down on the world, reigning
from the cross as from a throne. We think of his arms,
wide apart as they had to be, as stretched out towards
us sinners in appeal, and in invitation. For a hundred
reasons we ought to be grateful to our Lord for having
chosen, when he died for us, to die for us on a cross.

But there's one piece of symbolism about the cross
which is at once, I think, simpler than any other, and
more profound than any other. If someone asks you
for a recipe for drawing a picture of a cross, the best
answer is this, You've only got to write a capital I,
and then scratch it out. The capital I stands for self,
and the cross stands for capital I scratched out, for
self mortified.

You and I have each of us an I that is very dear to us,
a self which we think much more important than anything else in the world, which we are determined, at
all costs, to keep safe and comfortable if we can. That
is our natural instinct, to set up a great capital I in
front of our minds, and worship it. And the Christian
religion tells us that the real point of our life in this
world is to learn to do exactly the opposite. We want
to cancel that I, by drawing a line across it, by drawing
a cross across it. When you make the sign of the cross,
taking holy water or saying grace or on this other
occasion or that, think sometimes what it is you are
doing, what meaning it is that your action is symbol-
izing. You draw your hand down from forehead to

breast, and say to yourself, " Lord, here am I ". And then you draw your hand from shoulder to shoulder, and say, " Lord, scratch me out; teach me to mortify myself for your sake, to cancel myself for your sake, to become nothing, just nothing, for your sake ".

XII

Dead and buried

I DON'T know whether you learn any French history here. I can't remember ever being taught any French history in my life. But if you do learn any, you have probably by now got down as far as Clovis, who was king of the Franks in about A.D. 500. He was a pagan to start with, but was converted by marrying a Christian wife, St. Clotilde. And when he was being instructed before his baptism (by St. Remigius, I suppose) and had got down as far as the story of the Crucifixion, Clovis is said to have remarked, " If I had been there with my Franks, we wouldn't have stood for that sort of thing ". This is always quoted as the comment of a very stupid man, who quite failed to see the point. Well, I suppose he did, but in some ways I don't think it's such a bad comment. He was only an old tough, but he had the sense to see that this article in the Christian creed is a very extraordinary one—that the Crucifixion should ever have been *allowed* to happen.

I don't mean it was an extraordinary thing that MEN should have allowed it to happen. On the contrary, I'm afraid it was just like us all over; and if Clovis had really been there with his Franks, Pilate would probably have managed to explain to him that this was, after all, the best way out of a difficult situation. No, but it *was* extraordinary that the Son of God should be allowed to die. Our Lord, as we know, was free from original sin, and on that ground alone you might have thought he ought to be spared the sentence of death, which was only pronounced against our race because of Adam's fault. But there, of course, our Lady was in the same position; and she, like him, underwent the experience of death before she went home. But in our Lord's case there is a quite extraordinary paradox, which may be expressed quite simply in two words; God died. Oh, it's quite true that he didn't die *as God*; the Second Person of the Blessed Trinity could not, for a solitary moment of time, cease to exist. But the Person who breathed out his Spirit on the Cross was God; and yet he died.

We think of the Resurrection as an extraordinary thing; but that is really the wrong way to look at it. The Resurrection was, you may say, an inevitable event, an event which anybody ought to have foreseen. The pains of death, as St. Peter says, could not hold our Lord; of course they couldn't. No, the extraordinary thing was that the pains of death should ever, even for a moment, have the power to assail him. And yet they did. I've tried to explain to you, in one of my earlier sermons, why it was fitting that this should happen, so far as our limited intelligences can attempt to account for such a mystery. But, however much you or I may understand it or fail to understand it, there is the fact; God died. And it is a mystery which will, perhaps, make it easier for us to understand other mysteries; other mysteries which will cross the path of each of us, as life goes on. I mean, when someone for whom we care deeply is taken from us by death, and we find ourselves murmuring at the back of our minds the old complaint: " Why was this allowed to happen? " All we know is that God hung on the Cross, with his Blessed Mother beside him praying a Mother's prayers; and he was allowed to die.

Our Lord wasn't like other men. God didn't treat him as he treats you and me, sending what he sees best to us whether we like it or not, and often in spite of our frantic struggles to avoid it. No, nothing was done without the co-operation of our Lord's human will. And so it was at his death; his death was an *action*, not a pressure from outside which he couldn't avoid. Sometimes the deaths of holy people have the air of being deliberately willed. I was told a story of Father Bede Jarrett, the great Dominican provincial who died not very long ago, which illustrates that. I have been told that when he fell into his last illness, Father Bernard Delany went to see him, and said, " Well, Father, of course you know that you've got to get well; we can't possibly spare you ". And about a fortnight later, when Father Bernard went to see him again, Father Bede said, " Oh, Father, I'm so dreadfully tired; do you think you could let me want to die after all, or must I go on under obedience wanting to live? " And he naturally said, " Oh, of course I never meant to put you under *obedience* ". And Father Bede said, " Thank you so much ", and died about half an hour afterwards.

Well, as I say, nothing ever happened to our Lord which he didn't will with his human will, and therefore you may think of his death as an *action* of his; he didn't just get killed, or let himself die, he *chose* death. You get hints of that all through the story of the Crucifixion; that he should have died after three hours, I mean, whereas a man may hang alive on a cross for three days; that he should have cried aloud, saying quite intelligible words, a moment before, as if there was no mortal weakness in him; and then there's that phrase St. John uses, " Jesus, knowing that all things were now accomplished, that the scripture might be fulfilled, saith, I thirst "—he has the whole situation in his hands, up to the last moment. I don't mean that if our Lord's body had been submitted to a *post mortem* examination it would have been impossible to find any cause of death; I don't see why his death should have been supernatural in that sense. But his *will* co-operated in his own death; he was not robbed of his life, he deliberately handed it over.

It's curious, isn't it, how when you come to look into them all the clauses of the *Credo* which seemed the obvious and easy ones are really the obscure and difficult ones? To say that our Lord died seems quite an ordinary statement, but we have seen that it's a very extraordinary statement indeed. And then when we come on to this next clause, we're in just the same position. He died, and was buried; of course, you say, if he died, naturally the next thing was to bury him. Yes, but what I'm trying to show you is that, if it was an astonishing thing that our Lord should die, equally it was an astonishing thing that he should *stay dead*. The separation of body from soul, even in us ordinary human creatures, is not a natural state; it is an unnatural state which only takes effect because we are sinful creatures, fallen creatures, born under a curse. It's not natural for a soul to be separated from its body any more than it is natural for a fish to live out of water. And in our Lord's case there was no question of punishment for sin, no question of his having inherited the taint of fallen nature. Therefore you would have expected that as soon as he died he would come to life again. Every second during which he stayed dead, on Good Friday and Holy Saturday and Easter Sunday morning, was a kind of miracle; a much more remarkable miracle really than his Resurrection. Why did that happen?

You see, there's a very important principle in theology which lays it down that *miracula non sunt multiplicanda praeter necessitatem*. That is Latin, but it is not very difficult Latin to translate; I should think some of you could almost do it in your heads. MIRACULA, miracles, NON SUNT, are not, MULTIPLI-CANDA, meet to be multiplied, PRAETER, beyond, NECESSITATEM, what is necessary. God *can* do any amount of miracles, but we are not to assume that he throws miracles about the place recklessly all the time. For instance, if you look in your desk to find a parti-cular book and can't see it there, and the mistress says, " Go back and look again ", and you say a prayer to St. Anthony and find the book as soon as you open the desk, it's *possible* that there has been a miracle. It's possible that you left the book among the straw you put in your rabbit-hutch; there would be nothing unusual about that. And it's possible that St. Anthony found it there and scooped it up and put it back in your desk in answer to your prayer; St. Anthony is a very great saint, and it is not impossible that his intercession should have done that for you. But, on the principle which we have just been translating from the Latin, IT'S SAFER TO ASSUME that probably when you looked in your desk before you didn't look very carefully. And that makes us wonder why our Lord didn't come to life again almost immediately after he died, instead of lying on there in his tomb all Friday night, Saturday morning, Saturday afternoon, Saturday night, by a long *series*, as it were, of miracles. Why was it our Lord wanted, not merely to die, but to be buried in the earth?

Well, I think there are a whole lot of answers to that question; and we shall come across most of them in their due place, if we go on pegging away at the *Credo*. For instance, I think he wanted to fortify our imaginations against the uncomfortable feeling we all have when we go to a funeral, and the coffin is smothered in earth. We know REALLY that all that makes no difference, because the dead person will rise again; but there is something which depresses our imagination about the thought of a grave dug in the ground. To lighten that depression of ours, our Lord was content to be buried in a tomb, so that we should be able to think of the earth to which, sooner or later, we must return, as something which has been hallowed and quickened by his presence. When you were very small, and had to take medicine, did your mother ever take a sip of the medicine first, just so as to assure you that everything was all right? That is what Jesus Christ did, when he was buried for us. But we shall be talking about that, I suppose, when we get on to the Resurrection of the Flesh.

And then, I think he wanted his burial to be the mystical symbol of our baptism. St. Paul doesn't think of baptism so much as washing us *clean* from our sins; he likes to think of it rather as *burying* us *away* from our sins; the waters of baptism roll over us and engulf us, and we come to life again, as it were, new creatures, after that drowning. So, right back to St. Paul's time, Christian thought has looked upon our Lord's passage through the dark gates of the tomb as the type of our passage through the waters of baptism, and not merely the type of it, but the power which gives it its efficacy.

And then you've got to remember that, while his body lay in the tomb, our Lord's soul was not being idle. But we shall be talking about that, I hope, on the last Sunday of this term, so there's no need to deal with it now.

Meanwhile, there's a much more human reason our Lord had for putting a fairly long interval—not too long, but a fairly long interval—between his death and his rising again. He wanted, surely, to test the faith of his followers. I think that is a point we are apt to forget when we read the story of the Resurrection. I mean, when you read the story of the Resurrection don't you find yourself wondering how it was that it came as such a surprise to everybody? Why weren't they expecting it? He'd told them, again and again. Well, you know, it's only a guess, but I think it was partly the strain of waiting. Oh, it's quite true, our Lord hadn't merely told them he was going to rise from the dead; he had told them he was going to rise from the dead the third day. But hope deferred does make the heart sick; and you will find that the two disciples whom our Lord met on the road to Emmaus, that first Easter Day, talk as if they had grown tired of waiting. " And besides all this, it is now the third day since all this happened "—as if you couldn't be expected to wait a matter of forty-eight hours for God to bring his purpose to fulfilment. Our Lord wanted them, I think, to learn to wait; waiting is good for all of us.

And perhaps the simplest way of all to answer the question, " Why did our Lord want to be buried in the earth? " is this. He wanted the whole of his merciful design for our redemption to unroll itself gradually before our eyes, like a kind of slow-motion picture; never hurrying, never giving us the opportunity of saying, " Stop a minute, I haven't quite taken that in yet ". He wouldn't just come to earth, he would spend thirty-three years on earth. He wouldn't just appear suddenly and scatter miracles over the country-side in the course of an afternoon; he would spend three years going about and doing good. He wouldn't just die for us; he would hang there, three whole hours, on the Cross, so that we could watch him and take it all in. And he wouldn't just die-and-rise-again; he would spend part of three days in the tomb, with his enemies vindictively keeping watch over him, with his friends pathetically mourning for him, so that when the Resurrection did come it should come as a deliberate gesture. " I have power," he said, " to lay down my life, and power to take it up again." See how deliberately he lays aside that garment of life, master of the situation, even when his hands and feet are nailed to a cross! See how deliberately he takes that garment of life up again, master of the situation still, even when he lies in a tomb! Nothing impresses us so much, when we read the account of God's dealings with his creation, either in science or in history, as the majestic slowness of his movements. And God made Man did not lose the characteristics of Godhead; he went to work very slowly, for all the world to see that he was God.

XIII

Descendit ad inferos

WHEN I give out my text in Latin like that, it isn't
just a fit of absent-mindedness. I quite realize that,
other things being equal, it's more useful talking to
some of you, perhaps to most of you, in English than
in Latin. I'm only giving you this clause of the *Credo*
in Latin because the translation of it, to which we
are all accustomed, is a misleading one. " He
descended into hell," we say, without thinking much
about it. And what we ordinarily mean by hell is a
place or a state in which those who have died, ob-
stinately impenitent, are punished for all eternity.
There would be no sense in imagining that our Lord
descended into hell in that sense. He preached, we
are told, to the spirits in prison; but there wouldn't
be much point in that if the spirits were incapable of
repenting—as the souls in hell are incapable of
repenting—and therefore however much they were
preached to they could never get out. So I want to
make it clear at the start that our Lord didn't descend
ad infernum, into the place of everlasting punishment.
He descended *ad inferos,* to the people down below.
And if you want to know what is meant by the people
down below, you have to consider the usages of the
Hebrew language and the doctrine of the Church about
what happened to those who died before our Lord
came to earth.

The Hebrew word for hell, in our sense, is Gehenna. Our Lord, for example, tells us that it is better to enter into eternal life with a hand or a foot cut off than to have both hands and both feet and be cast into Gehenna. The Jews seem to have got the name from the Valley of Hinnom, close to Jerusalem, where they kept the city rubbish-heap. Most of you, I suppose, have never seen a rubbish-heap. But in the good old days, before salvage set in, when you had finished all the sardines in the tin and poured out the remains of the oil on your bread and butter, you didn't make up the tin into a neat parcel and send it to the salvage people; you threw it away. And wherever you got a rather steep valley, you would find that the people at the top end would throw all their old jam jars and umbrellas with broken ribs and so on down the valley, not caring much for the feelings of the people who lived at the bottom end. So it was with the valley of Hinnom; and the Jews, by an ingenious metaphor, thought of dead people who had lived very wicked lives as being thrown into a kind of super Valley of Hinnom, because dead people who had lived very wicked lives were good for nothing, like jam jars used to be before salvage was invented. That was Gehenna.

But when somebody died whose life had been more or less good, or perhaps indifferent, the Jews didn't think of them as having been thrown away into Gehenna; they thought of them as having gone down to Sheol, to the pit. And wherever you find the word " hell " used in the Old Testament, the Hebrew word for it is Sheol; which just meant the place where dead people go to.

The Hebrews, who had very vague ideas altogether about the future life, don't seem to have thought of Sheol as a particularly comfortable place or as a particularly uncomfortable place; it was just the world beneath. And when the *Credo* says that our Lord descended into hell it doesn't mean that he descended into Gehenna, into the place where wicked people are eternally punished. It means that he descended into Sheol, into the lower world, and preached, not to the souls of the damned, but to the souls of dead people who were in a kind of intermediate state. What was that intermediate state? How are we to think of it?

About one thing the teaching of the Church is quite clear: the holy patriarchs, people like Abraham and Isaac and Jacob, were not in hell at the time when our Lord came—not what we mean by hell—and they were not in heaven. They had to wait for our Lord's coming before they could get to heaven. And the place or the state in which they waited for Christ's coming is what we call Limbo. The reason why we call it by that odd name, which makes it sound like a patent soup, is I think because we are most familiar with it from the poet Dante, who wrote in Italian, and therefore we give it its Italian name. It's really a Latin word, *limbus*, which means the edge or the border of anything; the hem of your handkerchief, for example. And in theology it means a sort of borderline state, which is the only appropriate home of the borderline cases. Babies who die unbaptized, you see, are borderline cases; not being baptized, they have no right to heaven and yet as they haven't committed any sins they can't be sent to hell; therefore they go

to the *Limbus Infantium*, the Babies' Borderline State.
And the unbaptized babies, we are told, go on living
there for ever, not enjoying the beatific vision of God,
because they are not made to do that, but quite happy
all the same because they don't know what they've
missed. That's one kind of Limbo, which is permanent.

But there was another kind of Limbo, the *Limbus
Patrum*, the Patriarchs' Borderline State, in which holy
people like Abraham and Isaac and Jacob lived up till
Good Friday, A.D. 33. They, too, were borderline
cases. They were ear-marked for heaven, if I may put
it in that way, because they had looked forward, by
faith, to Christ's coming, and in that faith had lived
holy lives and gone on worshipping the true God.
What sins they had committed had already, somehow,
been expiated; they were ripe for heaven. But they
couldn't get to heaven till Jesus Christ died for our
sins; they had to wait, and the waiting-room assigned
to them was Limbo. I told you that the idea of
Gehenna was that of a rubbish-heap; in the same way,
if you like, you may think of Limbo as a lumber-
room, though the two words apparently are not connected. A lumber-room is a place where you keep
things which you don't need at the moment, but don't
want to throw away because you will need them later
on. So it was with the patriarchs; God didn't need
them yet in his drawing-room, so to speak, that is,
in heaven, but he would want them there later on,
so he didn't throw them away into Gehenna, the
rubbish heap; he kept them in Limbo, which is his
lumber-room.

If you were brought up in a fairly large house,

which had a lumber-room in the attics, I expect before now you have experienced the great thrill of exploring the lumber-room. Rather dark it was, so that you couldn't see very clearly what was what, and a good many of the things were covered up in dust-sheets, so that you had to poke about a good deal before you satisfied yourself that this was a roll of carpet, that this was the cage which the canary used to live in till the cat got it, that this was the rocking-horse which you remember standing in the nursery, and so on. What a pity it seemed that so many things were lying idle here, which might be made so useful downstairs: your father's old top-hat, which would do for drawing-room charades; and the concertina which did leak a bit, it's true, but still produced noises of a kind; and that large, ugly looking-glass, which might just as well be in your bedroom. And you went downstairs with your hands and face pretty dirty, but all worked up with this adventurous journey among the relics of the past.

Well, when our Lord Jesus Christ had died on the Cross, and left his body in the tomb to wait till Easter morning, the first thing which his spirit did was—what? To explore his Father's lumber-room. He went to Limbo, and visited all the borderline cases of the old patriarchs who had been waiting so many centuries for him to come. How they must have crowded round him, and what a lot he must have explained to them which they hadn't been able to understand properly hitherto! " It's all right, Adam (he will have said), you did a very foolish thing, and a very wicked thing, when you ate the fruit of the tree although you had been told not to; but I have been hanging, from twelve to three this afternoon, on a very different kind of tree, and now the world has been redeemed from the consequences of your sin. It's all right, Eve; you disobeyed, but my Mother, by her obedience, has brought salvation into the world, as you brought sin into the world. You see now, Noe, what was the idea of building an ark to save yourself and your family from the flood? It was a prophecy of the Church which I am just going to found, the ark which stays afloat in a sinful world, and saves men's souls from being engulfed in it. You, Abraham, when you sacrificed your son Isaac, or rather were prepared to sacrifice him, were doing what my heavenly Father did when he sent me into the world to die. Your ladder, Jacob, set up between earth and heaven, was the image of my Incarnation; you, Joseph, were sold for twenty pieces of silver, I was sold for thirty. Do you remember, Moses, how you set up a brazen serpent on a pole in the wilderness, and all the people who had been bitten by the snakes, if only they could be persuaded to look up at it, got well? That is what my Cross is going to do now for sinners." And so on, all down the list of the holy people whom we read about in the Old Testament. What a holiday that must have been for them all, when our Lord came and explained to them, at last, what their experiences in life had meant, and ended up, " Now you are going home with me; it is time you went home! "

All that we mean, when we say that our Lord descended to the people beneath. He didn't descend to Gehenna; but he descended to Limbo, and preached to the holy patriarchs who were waiting for him there. But now, is that all we mean by our Lord's descent into the lower world? I don't think you can say that the teaching of the Church is very clear beyond that; God's revelation doesn't tell us very much, for certain, about a future world. But if you will look at that odd passage in the first epistle of St. Peter, where he refers to this event, you will find a hint, I think, of a further meaning in the doctrine we are considering. He tells us that our Lord, in his spirit, " went and preached to the spirits who lay in prison. Long before, they had refused belief, hoping that God would be patient with them, in the days of Noe ". And, he adds, a few verses lower down, " that is why dead men, too, had the gospel message brought to them; though their mortal natures had paid the penalty in men's eyes, in the sight of God their spirits were to live on ". That passage raises a lot of difficulties. Why does St. Peter concentrate entirely on the people who lived at the time of the Flood, when there were so many millions of other dead people to be considered? Who were the people who had refused belief in the time of Noe, and if they refused belief, why didn't they go to hell? And what is all this about their paying the penalty in men's eyes, and their spirits living on in the sight of God?

I can only suggest briefly how I should explain the passage, which is a very difficult passage indeed. I think St. Peter concentrates upon the contemporaries of Noe, because in the days of Noe the world was very wicked—that was why the flood happened. And the people who refused belief were the people who wouldn't take any notice when Noe told them there was going to be a great deluge, and they had better take cover somewhere. The book of Genesis doesn't tell us anything about what other people thought or said when Noe began to build the Ark, or when it rained and rained and it began to look as if Noe hadn't been wrong after all. I think what St. Peter means us to see is that there were, even in those wicked days, some people who hadn't enough faith to go into the Ark when Noe did, and yet weren't altogether wicked people. What became of them? They were drowned by the flood, sure enough; they paid the penalty in their mortal natures. But when they were drowned, they didn't go to hell; their spirits lived on in the sight of God. And to these people, who were not wicked enough to go to hell, and hadn't got enough faith to go to Limbo, our Lord, in his spirit, went and preached. When it says he preached to them, it only means, I think, that he brought them the good news of the salvation which his Cross had given to the world. Not in Gehenna, not in Limbo—where were they, then? Surely in Purgatory; in a place or state where they underwent punishment for their sins, but were destined later to go to heaven; only that couldn't happen till our Lord had died to redeem them; and many of them no doubt weren't yet ready for heaven, even then.

If that is the true explanation of what St. Peter means, then it follows that Purgatory, too, as well as Limbo, was visited by our Lord in that royal progress of his on Good Friday and Holy Saturday. And with his coming a new hope came to the souls in Purgatory and has remained there ever since. They were souls bound for heaven. What light, what rest was given to them when our Lord came and told them that! If you and I go to Purgatory, we may have much to suffer there, but it will not be a place of despair or of doubt. We shall be able to say, *Descendit ad inferos*; Jesus Christ has been here, and he has made a door in this prison house through which, not now but later on, I shall follow him to heaven.

XIV

The third day he rose again from the dead

TODAY, I shall have to cram a good deal into my sermon. I shan't be preaching to you again till the Sunday after next, when I want to talk to you about the Ascension, because it will be topical. So I've only just these twenty minutes in which to point out to you the enormous place which the Resurrection of Jesus Christ holds in our theology. In three ways especially it is important. It was the climax of that series of miracles by which our Lord justified his claim to be the ambassador of a Divine revelation. It was an assurance to us, once for all, that our race had triumphed over death. And it was the type and the inspiration of that rising again to new life which sacramental grace makes possible to us. It was a proof; it was a hope; it was a challenge.

Don't let's make any mistake about this; he claimed to do miracles, and claimed, by doing miracles, to prove where he came from; to prove that he came straight from God. Of course nowadays people aren't too keen about the Gospel miracles. They have an odd sort of feeling that it would be rather vulgar to multiply loaves in the wilderness, rather bad form to turn water into wine. They will tell you that that may be all very well, but for themselves they prefer to think of Jesus of Nazareth simply as somebody

who went about doing good. If anybody ever talks
to you like that, turn on them at once with the
question, " Yes, and what good exactly did he do?
Do we ever read of his meeting an old woman carrying
a heavy burden up a hill, and offering to carry it up
for her? Did he ever jump into the water to save
anybody's life? Do we ever hear of his distributing
money among starving people? Did he go round
comforting the sick, and telling them to bear up?
No, there is no trace of all that. He didn't jump into
the water, he walked on the water. When people were
hungry, he didn't distribute *money*, he distributed
bread, miraculously multiplied. He didn't *comfort*
the sick, he *healed* them. What you mean, you
mutton-headed old fool, when you say that he went
about doing good is that he went about doing miracles.
There's lots of evidence of that; none of the other
thing ".

And he wasn't content to save people from the
danger of death by drowning, or hunger, or disease;
he raised people from the dead. How many times?
Admirably instructed as you are in Scripture studies,
you are all burning to give me the answer: three times.
And you are all wrong. Not three times, but four. He
raised Jairus' daughter. He raised the widow's son at
Naim. He raised Lazarus. And finally he raised
himself. You hadn't thought of that; but of all his
miracles, that was the greatest. Jairus' daughter, just
dead, only a moment or two ago. The widow's son,
already being carried out to his funeral. Lazarus,
when he had been four days in the tomb. But there
was a climax still to come. What if he should raise
to life a man who had died on a cross, and was stabbed

with a spear to make certain, and buried in a grave behind a great sealed door of stone, guarded by soldiers, and that man himself?

He had told his enemies that he would. He had said, " Destroy this temple, and in three days I will raise it again "; and I suppose when he said that he pointed to himself. The Jews professed to misunderstand him, professed to think he was talking about Herod's temple. But they knew really, and they remembered all about it. As soon as he was dead they went to Pilate and asked that the tomb might be guarded. " Sir, we remember that this deceiver said, After three days I will rise again." They had understood, and accepted the challenge, and when the tomb was found empty, if they'd been even sportsmen, they would have owned that they were beaten. But they had to put up a story about his being taken away in the night; that was the best they could manage. The Cross was the crucial experiment by which they had decided to test whether they could put an end to his miracles by murdering him; and the test went against them. That is one meaning, and a very important meaning, of Easter Day.

But at the same time he met a much older, a much more formidable challenge. He settled, once for all, the old struggle, the old tug-of-war, you may call it, between life and death. It is a battle fought out under our eyes, if we take the trouble to look, every spring and every autumn; the battle between Life and Death in nature. Which is really the more powerful of the two? Which is destined, in the long run, to swallow up the other? Every autumn, Death can say to Life, " You'll excuse my saying so, but I seem to have made you look a bit of a fool. What's become of all your spring fashions now? Where are your geraniums, where is your honeysuckle, where are your artichokes?" Of course, there are a few evergreens that confuse the reckoning, ivy and holly and the aspidistras in people's front windows; but for practical purposes Death can claim, every autumn, to have swept the board. And Life has no answer, except to say, "Just you wait". And they wait, till spring comes; and then Life can point proudly round the battle-field of nature and say, "There are my geraniums! There is my honeysuckle! There are my artichokes! Did you think you'd killed them? More fool you, if you did". And so the old business begins again, year after year. It's like a perpetual deuce-game at tennis; vantage-in every May, and vantage-out every November.

But, meanwhile, there's this to be considered—Life has to go on producing fresh specimens of the type; it can't re-create the old ones. The geranium in that corner of the bed isn't the same as the geranium that grew there last year. Last year's geranium went on to the bonfire, or perhaps it's pressed in between the leaves of your album; it's a new geranium that has come up instead. The artichoke that is coming up just there isn't the same as the artichoke that came up just there last year; last year's artichoke went inside you; it's a new artichoke this year. So, you see, Life wins on the whole over the species; the species is indestructible. Let Death do what he may, geraniums still go on, and artichokes still go on. But the *individual* perishes; *that* geranium will never be worn in a button-hole again; *that* artichoke will never be eaten with melted butter again. And there is one species in nature which has, for us, a unique interest; even more interest than artichokes: what about man? Men, too, are born and die; every time you pick up a copy of *The Times* you see a long list of new people who have arrived, and then a long list of the people who are dead. The species goes on, but what about the individual? Does Death triumph here, too? Does immortality belong only to the race, or can the individual human being look forward, somehow, to immortality?

That issue, too, was fought out on a spring morning. There's a fascinating verse of St. Matthew, just after his description of how St. Joseph of Arimathea took our Lord's body and buried it. " But there were two who sat on opposite the tomb, Mary Magdalen and the other Mary with her." They cannot drag themselves away, spectators of the great world-conflict between life and death, which has now reached its final round. If nothing happens on Easter Morning, then it is all over; there is no hope left for human hearts. *Mors et vita duello conflixere mirando*, says the Easter sequence; " Life and Death met in wondrous combat ". And the darkness fell, and the sabbath dawned; and you were not allowed to go out and look at the tomb on the sabbath. But as soon as the grey twilight of Sunday morning came, Mary Magdalen and the other Mary were there, with their spices. And they looked, to find the stone rolled away, and the soldiers asleep, and the tomb empty.

We speak of our Lord's Resurrection as the greatest of his miracles; but in a sense it was not a miracle at all. He simply did, on Easter Day, what we shall all do at the Last Judgement, rose again with his Body.

That he should be able to pass out of the tomb, leaving the stone and the seal undisturbed, that he should be able to enter the cenacle when the doors were locked, was only natural; his Risen Body was simply obeying the law of risen bodies. What was much more wonderful, though it's curious to think of it, is that he should have eaten a meal with his apostles after he had risen again. It was only by a special and a miraculous disposition of Providence that he did that; it is not the nature of a risen body to be supported by food. He ate and drank with his apostles to convince them that he had really risen; once and perhaps twice. But for the most part, during those forty days, his Body will, as I say, have obeyed the law of risen bodies; it was now glorified. He wanted to show himself to us as the first-born from the dead; he wanted to assure us that we shall be, one day, as he was then. All of us will rise, even impenitent sinners. But we can welcome, in a special way, the assurance that those who belong to his mystical Body will, by that very fact, share his immortality. We can think of those whom we loved, and who have now been taken from us, as united, now, with him, and only waiting for his bidding before they rise again, glorified with the same glory which shone out in the risen Christ.

Meanwhile, there is a third point to be considered. Easter does not only mean the culminating proof of our Lord's Divine Mission, does not only mean the hope of immortality. It means that you and I, baptized Christians, are living here and now with a risen life; we are dead to sin, we have risen with Christ. St. Paul is always rubbing that in. " Buried with him in baptism; in whom also you are risen again "—what does he mean when he talks like that, " buried in baptism "? Well, of course you have to remember that the ceremonies of baptism nowadays aren't quite what they were in St. Paul's time. When I baptized Charles Acton last term, I didn't plunge him into a large bath full of water. Just as well that I didn't because he howled quite enough as it was. But in St. Paul's time the people who were baptized were mostly grown-ups, and they (as a rule) were baptized by complete immersion; you went into the river Jordan, or some other piece of water that was handy, and the priest who was baptizing you gave you a ducking. And the symbolical meaning of that was that you were being buried, as it were, under the water; you died and were buried and rose again, in union with the death and burial and resurrection of Jesus Christ. And when you came up out of the water you were a new person altogether, your old self had died, and a new person had come to life instead.

You can't begin to understand St. Paul's epistles until you realize that that was the way in which he thought of baptism. Nowadays, of course, we think of baptism more as washing us clean from our sins. But, if that were all, why should it be impossible for us to be baptized twice, or indeed as often as we liked? Washing is a ceremony which can be repeated; if one of the nuns tells you to go and wash your face, you don't say, " I'm afraid that's impossible; I've washed it already ". No, the thing that can't be repeated is this business of death and resurrection. And that's what happened to you, you see, when you were christened; you died to your old self, to the sinful nature which you inherited as a child of Adam, and became a new creature, the child of Christ.

You and I, more's the pity, haven't kept our baptismal innocence. We have sinned, and we go on sinning, and that is why we have to go to confession at intervals; that's washing if you like. But at the root of it all, you see, baptism has made a permanent difference; we are no longer what we were. The devil had a natural claim over us, so to speak, until the day when we were christened; now he hasn't, now it is Christ who has the natural claim over us. Life has triumphed over death in our souls. Grace has been implanted in us, a principle of supernatural life, a seed that sprang from our Lord's tomb. That garden of the Resurrection was the nursery garden of the whole Church. And that's why we must never allow ourselves to grow despondent over our sins, even when we find ourselves falling into them again and again; there's something in us stronger than sin, Divine grace, which is always thrusting up like a plant rooted in our souls, always claiming us for itself. There is no autumn in your soul; as long as you believe in Jesus Christ and in what his Resurrection has done for you, it is always spring.

And just as Christ, by rising again, has planted this irresistible principle of victory in your soul and mine, so by his rising again he has planted an irresistible principle of victory in his Church. Again and again, when you read the history of the Church, you will come across periods when it looks as if the whole thing was no use, and there was nothing for her but to chuck up the sponge; the world keeps on persecuting her, and it seems bound to get her down. You see it in the Dark Ages, when the barbarians invaded Europe; you see it at the time of the Reformation, when half of Europe was torn away from her influence; you see it at the time of the Napoleonic Wars, when it looked for a moment as if religion had ceased to count. You will live your life, maybe, in equally troubled times, when it will look as if everything we Catholics care for were going under. But the Church is the Church of the Risen Christ, and till the end of time every death she undergoes will be the prelude to a resurrection.

XV

He ascended into heaven, sitteth at the right hand of God

THIS IS in some ways the least surprising of all the clauses in the *Credo*. Having risen from the dead, our Lord proceeded to ascend into heaven; after all, he couldn't very well have done anything else. Long ago, when I was a Church of England clergyman, and used to bother rather about what other Church of England clergymen thought, the extraordinary theological views they would produce, I noticed this curious thing—that it was quite common to find people who said they believed in the Resurrection but didn't believe in the Ascension. I used to ask them, but I could never get any intelligible answer, What DID they think had happened? Here is the Body of our Lord Jesus Christ raised from the tomb; we've admitted that. What, then, was its later history? Did they think that our Lord went on, not for forty days, but for perhaps forty years, in hiding; and at the end of that period he died and was buried like the rest of us? Or did they think that our Lord's Body was annihilated, by some special decree of Providence? Unless you believed either one or the other of those two very improbable stories, you were *forced* to believe that our Lord had ascended into heaven. Even if the Gospels had told us nothing about the circumstances of it, we should know that our Lord had ascended, simply because he isn't here. So let us have no nonsense about that; if we believe all the *Credo* has had to tell us so far, this new clause in it is as easy as pie. He ascended into heaven; naturally; what else could he do? He is sitting at the right hand of the Father; of course he is; what on earth would be the sense of looking for him anywhere else?

No, the odd thing here, the thing that wants explaining here, is that he should have wanted to wait forty days on earth before he ascended into heaven. It was very fortunate for you, of course, that he did, because it means your getting a nice holiday in the middle of the summer term, just when holidays are worth having. But suppose for a moment that the Gospels had told us nothing about what happened after our Lord's burial, except the bare facts, as the Creed records them for us, that he rose again from the dead the third day and ascended into heaven—if that were all we knew from the Gospels, and if Catholic tradition had told us nothing more about it, what picture should we naturally form in our minds about what had happened? We should imagine, shouldn't we, that he had mustered together all his followers—there were only so few of them, remember, only a hundred and twenty of them—on the afternoon, say, of Easter Day, perhaps in the cenacle, perhaps out of doors on the Mount of Olives or somewhere like that; that he had said good-bye to them, and told them to go out and preach his gospel, and then had disappeared into the clouds. All that on Easter Day; why should he wait till later on? Well, we know that he *did* stay on earth forty days, and I think if we look at the fragmentary notices of what he did during those forty days we shall get some idea of what the delay was for.

In the first place, it was important that his disciples should be good witnesses of the Resurrection, of the fact that it had happened. And, you know, a person who is going through a very exciting experience, who receives unexpectedly a piece of very important news, good or bad, isn't in a very favourable position for describing afterwards exactly what happened. The effect of a shock like that is to stun the mind, and it seems that when the mind is stunned the memory doesn't function very reasonably. I don't mean that one remembers *nothing* on such occasions; what happens is rather that you notice and remember a whole lot of idiotic little details, and forget all the things that were important. For instance, if you get married, you'll probably find yourself in a sort of dazed condition on your wedding-day, being pushed about by bridesmaids and sacristans and registrars without any very clear idea of what you're doing except a general sense that it's important to keep smiling, especially when the photographers are about. And if you were questioned, afterwards, about your wedding-day, you would probably remember exactly what the bridesmaids wore and how the best man's collar came loose from his shirt at the back, but quite vague about whether you said " I will " or " I won't ". If our Lord had ascended to heaven immediately after his Resurrection, it would have left, according to all human probabilities, a sort of blurred impression on the minds of the people who saw it; and if somebody had asked them afterwards, " Are you certain you didn't dream all this? " they would have had to say, " Well, I don't think I did; but of course it's all very confused in my mind, after all these years ". So our Lord wasn't going to have it like that. He was going to have St. Thomas absent on the first occasion when he rejoined his Apostles; so that St. Thomas would go about saying, " Of course, I quite understand you people getting worked up about it, after all we've been through; but it's quite clear to *me* that you have seen a ghost ". And then, Low Sunday, and the print of the nails. . . . They were to have forty days of his company; in the first place, so that they could make quite *sure*.

And in the second place, I think, so that the parting should be gradual, not sudden. That is obviously the true explanation of a scene which we are all apt to get wrong, because our Bible gives us such a bad translation of it. When our Lord met St. Mary Magdalen in the garden, we are expected to believe that he said, " Touch me not, because I have not yet ascended to my Father·". If he had said that, it would have been rather cruel, and he would have been talking utter nonsense. Why on earth should the fact that he had not yet ascended be a *reason* for not touching him? No, St. Mary Magdalen has fallen at his feet and is clinging to them; you get that picture in St. Matthew. And our Lord didn't say, " Touch me not "; anybody who knows any Greek at all will tell you that what he said was, " Stop clinging to me like that. . . . Stop clinging to me like that, as if you wanted to keep me chained to earth, and were afraid that I should leave you; it is all right,

I have not ascended to my Father yet; you will be seeing more of me ". Our Lord, you see, was always so nice to his friends. He knew that it was going to be a great wrench for them when he went back to his Father and left them to live on in the world without him. So he condescended to their weakness, and let them have forty days, still, of his company. Let's try to remember that about our Lord if we ever find that our friends are being rather tiresome and soppy about this business of saying good-bye. Let's humour them, as our Lord did, by not being in too much of a hurry to get the business of parting over; let's not make things too sudden for them, if we can help it.

And there was a third reason why our Lord stayed on on earth for a bit; and that was because his disciples were so stupid. Right up to the Last Supper they were always getting things wrong when he tried to teach them their theology; and now they had all run away and deserted him—how could they be certain what he meant them to do next? So he had to tell them very carefully, " Go and teach all nations, baptizing them in the name of the Father and of the Son and of the Holy Ghost. Whose sins you remit, they are remitted to them, and whose sins you retain, they are retained ". And then to St. Peter, " Feed my sheep "; and so on. For forty days, St. Luke tells us, he was with them telling them about the things which pertained to the kingdom of God—that is, to his Church. And you've got to remember that he evidently told them things in the course of those forty days which, as far as we know, he had never told them before. About Confirmation, for example; nothing is said about Confirmation in any of the

Gospels, and yet if you read the Acts of the Apostles you will see that it is a ceremony as old as Baptism.

For those reasons, then, our Lord stayed forty days on earth, mostly in Galilee, I expect, where the apostles could recover memories of the past, and where there was more chance of being alone with him. Then, it seems, they went back to Jerusalem; and one day he got them to come with him to the mount of Olives, where he was taken up into heaven, and a cloud received him out of their sight. Who was there? We don't know, exactly; St. Bede's hymn talks as if our Lady had been there, and she is generally there in the pictures, but we don't really *know*; all we know is that the eleven Apostles were there. When it says that our Lord went up into the sky, does that mean that we are to think of heaven as somewhere up in the air? Well, we can if we like; but I imagine that only gives us a very imperfect picture of the truth. When we talk of going down to hell, we don't really mean that if you got hold of one of those electric drills the men make such a noise with in the street and burrowed and burrowed and burrowed till you thought you must be nearly getting to New Zealand, you would come across hell. We can't be certain, of course, because nobody's tried; but I think most people would tell you that going " down " to hell is probably a metaphor. And in the same way, if you invented an aeroplane, or I suppose you would have to call it a spaceoplane, which could go up and up and up without stopping, there's no reason to think you would ultimately get to heaven. Heaven *may* be accurately thought of as up in the air; but I think it's really better to remind ourselves that all our ideas about space and position in space are the ideas of human creatures, whose thought can only move in three dimensions at the best of times, and has been a good deal confused by Einstein on the top of it.

When he ascended, our Lord really passed, surely, into a quite different kind of existence, in which, for all we know, our notions about space and position in space may have no meaning. All we know from the eye-witnesses is that our Lord went up into the air and was hidden from sight by a cloud; what happened behind that cloud we shan't know until we, too, have left earth behind us.

Well, that gets the history of the Ascension clear, and the meaning of the Ascension clear; and now, what is the *moral* of the Ascension? I suppose you could put it in plenty of different ways; but I think the nicest way of looking at it is the way a certain Père Clugny (I think it was) used to look at it, one of the many very holy priests whom France produced in the seventeenth century. He used to say that the Ascension was his favourite mystery among all the mysteries of our Lord's life, because it was the only one which made you think how nice it was for our Lord, instead of thinking how nice it was for *us*. The Nativity, you see, was a day of great joy for us, but not for our Lord, in that cold stable. The Passion and the Crucifixion are things we cannot think of without tears of gratitude, but they brought nothing except anguish and misery to our Lord. Even his Resurrection, though it was a day of joy for him, was still *more* a day of joy for us—our sins forgiven, the fear of death for ever dispelled; we are glad on Easter Day, but it's rather a selfish kind of gladness, or so

Père Clugny thought. But the Ascension—there at last we get the opportunity of quite unselfish rejoicing; of being glad that our Lord is going back home to his Father, and forgetting what it means to us, that we shall not see him, not hear his gracious accents, any longer. We can say to him, " How I wish you had stayed on earth, so that *we* could have been like the Apostles, and seen you, and talked to you! But I'm glad you went up to heaven, because now you are in glory, and it would be impossible for anyone who loves you as I love you to grudge you any moment of that! "

And at the same time it's splendid to realize that our Lord Jesus Christ is sitting, now, at the right hand of God. Oh yes, it's quite true, we've sailed off into metaphors again. Why " sitting " at the right hand of God? St. Stephen, at the moment of his martyrdom, saw our Lord *standing* at the right hand of God; isn't that rather confusing? No, not really, because we are using metaphors. To Stephen, in his vision, our Lord appeared standing up, as if starting up from his throne to meet his first martyr; more ordinarily we think of our Lord as seated, because he is at rest, now, from his labours, because he rules, now, over Creation. But it's all a metaphor; so for that matter is the " right hand " of God. When you grow up and have to entertain people at dinner, you will have to be very careful to put the most important person on your right. It's not always easy if you are the kind of person who can't tell your right from your left except by the vaccination mark. But always, for some reason, the important person is on the right. So we think of our Lord at the right hand of God, because we want to think of him as higher than anything else; higher, for example, than the holy angels. Close to God, with a closeness you and I cannot imagine, reigns eternally one who is a man of our own flesh and blood, who knows what it feels like to suffer and to be tempted, who is proud of us because we belong to him, who wants us to follow him to heaven and be near him; near, through him, to his heavenly Father.

So we don't, as you might expect, make Ascension Day a day of fasting and mourning, the day on which our best Friend was taken away from us. We rejoice, for his sake, that he has left this miserable world behind, to enjoy eternity; we rejoice, for our own sakes, because in him humanity has stormed the citadels of heaven; because he, who once beckoned us to share in his suffering, beckons us now to share in his glory.

XVI

From thence he shall come to judge the
living and the dead

THE DOCTRINE of the Last Judgement comes naturally
to us, for several reasons. For one thing, there is such
a lot about it in the New Testament. Much more,
you know, than most people imagine; most people
haven't read, for example, the epistles very carefully.
I should hazard the guess that you won't easily find
a chapter in any of the epistles, whether those written
by St. Paul or those of his fellow-Apostles, in which
the second coming of our Lord is not referred to. You
see, it is clear that our Lord refused to tell his disciples
when the second coming was going to happen, and he
left them still guessing. They were not in a position
to say that it *would* happen in their own life-time; on
the other hand, there was no reason for asserting that
it *wouldn't* happen in their life-time. It's true, our
Lord had said that his Gospel would be preached
to the whole world before the end came; but then,
you see, the Gospel did get preached, in a sur-
prisingly short space of time, all over what was then
the known world. It hadn't been preached in
America or Australia, but then in those days they
didn't know that America or Australia existed, and
somehow managed to get on quite cheerfully without
them.

If I may put it very vulgarly, I don't think the Christians of the first century thought the betting was on the Last Judgement finding them still alive. But they felt the betting was even—and so it was; it might quite well have happened in the first century. And the betting is still even today; only because of the long lapse of time since our Lord was on earth we have come to assume, quite irrationally, that it *won't* happen in our lifetime. It isn't as *real* to us as it was to the first Christians. When *they* talked about our Lord coming to judge the living and the dead, they meant he would judge the dead as well as the living. When *we* talk about it, we mean that he will come to judge the living as well as the dead. But still, you've evidently got to believe in a doctrine which was so clearly popular in the early Church, which was so clearly taught, for that matter, by our Lord himself.

And another reason why this doctrine comes so naturally to us is because we've so often seen pictures of it. That, I think, is chiefly due to the fact that a great many artists found it a jolly subject to paint. You could get in such a lot of people, and it was so easy to know what expressions to give them, the good on one side looking up into the air with a holy sort of expression, and the wicked balancing them on the other side of the picture, all looking terribly frightened and despairing. And besides the people you could get in angels blowing trumpets, and devils doing some very useful work with pikles. And if you were a medieval artist, you spread yourself on painting in portraits of the people you didn't like much, and putting them among the lost souls on the left, including, probably, a portrait of your diocesan bishop which nobody could possibly mistake.

And the third reason why the doctrine of the Last Judgement comes easy to us, at least while we are at school, is because we are accustomed to the term ending up with examinations, so it's natural to think of the world as coming to an end in the same way, with a kind of general showdown. Like the Oxford undergraduate I think I told you about when I gave you your retreat, who dreamed that he saw the ten commandments stuck up on a notice-board with a direction at the top which said, " Not more than five of these should be attempted ". We're so accustomed to asking ourselves whether it's worth while going and having a bathe on a splendid hot day, when it MAY mean we shan't know the dates of the kings of England a month hence, that we turn that into a parable of our whole lives, and think of the world as a sunshiny day clouded by one shadow—the shadow of the judgement. That, I may say in passing, is a rotten way to go about the business of religion. It makes you think of this very deceptive and transitory world as fun, and religion as a drawback; instead of realizing what religion is—a tremendous adventure which makes even this very deceptive and transitory world worth living in, because it is shot through with the glory of God and the love of Jesus Christ.

But, when we've said that we find it natural to think of the world as ending in a showdown, we mustn't refuse to notice that there are certain difficulties about this doctrine. I don't mean that it's difficult to *believe* in, but it's difficult, rather, to *understand*. In the first place, why should it be necessary to have a last judgement at all? Because we shall all have been judged already, as we know, at the moment after death. Of course, there were old-fashioned Protestants who used to think of people's souls, as well as their bodies, going to sleep until the General Resurrection at the end of the world, so that there was no particular judgement at all, and no need for one. When you died, it was like going to sleep in a train, somewhere in the middle of Worcestershire, and waking up at Paddington; waking up with all the trumpets and the shouting going on. Well, of course that won't do, because you've got to leave room for Purgatory. Purgatory is going on now, so is heaven, so is hell. What happens at the last judgement is that our souls are rejoined by our bodies; although (as St. Paul assures us) those bodies will now be heavenly bodies, quite unlike the bodies we wear now, yet in some mysterious way the same. But our souls will already have been experiencing eternity, it may be for centuries, before the last judgement happens. What is the use, then, of there being a last judgement at all, when we have already had a particular judgement which decided our eternity? It seems *untidy* somehow; rather like the Government issuing new ration books when we had all got ration books already.

I don't think there is any answer to that difficulty given in the ordinary books of theology. What I am telling you now is therefore simply my own guess, my own impression of what the reason for it may be. I think God wants us, when he brings this material creation of his to an end, to see the whole history of it set out, and set out as it really is—a gigantic struggle between good and evil. We shall see where we fitted into the pattern, what infinitesimal contribution we made, each of us, to the good and the evil in the world. At our particular judgement, I suppose, each of us will see his or her own life as the biography of a solitary unit; at the general judgement we shall read the story again as it fits into a vast history, the history of mankind. And we shall see, I imagine, how other people fitted into the pattern, too, people we were interested in. And we shall see exactly how God was right, and exactly how right God was, not merely in his way of treating us, but in his way of treating everybody; the chances he gave them, the patience he exercised over their sins, the eternity to which he consigned them. Every clue will be unravelled; it will be like the end of a really good novel, a detective story if you like, where everything at last fits into its place. That, I think, is the most sensible idea you can have of what the last judgement will be like.

But then, there's a second difficulty, and it's one which doesn't apply only to the general judgement, it applies to the particular judgement equally. Why does God need to judge us at all? When a person is brought to trial by English law, what is the point of all that business of people dressing up in wigs and saying " Melud " to one another? The idea is that the judge, who doesn't know whether John Smith stole the diamond tiara or not, can find out the truth—or rather, make the jury feel satisfied that they have found out the truth. It's the same with those examinations we were talking about; I'm sorry to harp on them so much, but they do illustrate the point, don't they? The idea of these examinations is to find out whether you've been working or not; that is what the examiner wants to *know*. He might, of course, just ask you, mightn't he? But that way of doing things would be open to certain abuses. So he examines you, by way of finding out what he wants to know.

Well, when we talk about *God judging us*, these considerations don't apply. We can't imagine God not *knowing* what sort of lives we have led in the world; and if he knows, how can he want to find out? And if he doesn't want to find out, what is the point of judging us? You know, that objection is perfectly well found. God doesn't need, in the strict sense, to judge us when we are dead, because he knows already exactly what the state of our soul is. You may say, if you will, that he is judging us at every moment of our lives; he is judging me now as I stand here, judging you as you sit there. You don't need to think of him as prying and poking about to see what sort of person you are; he knows it with a direct glance. Think of a person who knows how to do it steering a boat; you probably don't, nor do I much. But the person who does know how to steer can feel, at every moment, just how the boat is answering her helm. He doesn't need to look about and see which way she is heading; he can feel it by every slight pressure on the rudder. So Almighty God holds your soul in his hand all the time; can tell at every moment, as you react to this or that temptation, this or that grace he gives you, exactly how far you are keeping true to him, answering your helm. And therefore when we say that God will judge your soul after death, we are using a metaphor, just as much as we are using a metaphor when we say that our Lord is " sitting at the right hand of the Father ".

What is it that we mean, then, by this metaphor of judgement? Why, surely this—that immediately after death the exact state of your soul will be made clear, not for God's benefit, but for your own. In our earthly judgements, in our earthly examinations, it is the other way round. John Smith knows whether he has stolen the diamond tiara or not, but the judge doesn't, not yet. You know (if you will be honest with yourself) whether you have been putting in a good term's work or not, but the examiner doesn't, not yet. Whereas, when you die, God will know exactly what the state of your soul is, but you won't, not yet. It's as if you were to come to me on a Saturday evening and say, " Bless me, Father, for I have sinned ", and I were to say, " Yes, I know you have, you've done this and that and that ". Some of the Saints, we are told, used to read people's consciences like that; St. John Bosco, for example, and the dear Curé d'Ars; and very convenient it would be, because you wouldn't have to go to the trouble of examining your conscience before you came into the confessional. Well, that is what your judgement will be like. God won't have to find out what you have done and what the state of your soul is; he will know, and he will communicate that knowledge to you. You will be flooded all at once by a full realization of the kind of person you are, and whether you are due for heaven, and if so, what sort of Purgatory you have to expect before you get there. And so it will be at the general judgement—God won't find out anything he didn't know before. He will simply make it clear to mankind what it is that has been happening all along; which souls were true to him and which weren't, and why.

But there is one further question to be asked about this item in the *Credo*, which I dare say you have been wanting to point out to me for some time. The *Credo* doesn't say God will judge us, it says Jesus Christ will come to judge us. And evidently it means Jesus Christ as man will come to judge us, because it is all part, as it were, of his human biography. Now what exactly is the point of that? Why, surely this, that what we shall be judged by is our reaction to the love of Jesus Christ and his offer of salvation. We needn't stop to consider now the people who didn't know about the love of Jesus Christ, who hadn't any chance of understanding about the love of Jesus Christ; they will be judged, and we must suppose on some principle we have no means of guessing at. But people like you and me, who have been brought in contact with the love of Jesus Christ, how did we react to it? According as we have accepted or rejected it, we shall be, in the hour of judgement, what we are.

And therefore it will be Jesus Christ who judges us. He was to come into the world twice, and both times, he has told us himself, it was for judgement. That is what Simeon meant when he told our Lady, " This child is destined for the rise and the fall (that is the salvation or the condemnation) of many in Israel, that the thoughts of many hearts may be revealed ". Our Lord was sitting in judgement, all the time, on his fellow-men; when he stood before Pilate, it was Christ who judged Pilate, not Pilate Christ. But his judgement was being formed, not pronounced yet; it was a secret judgement. So it is when he comes to you and me in Holy Communion; he is judging us all the time; that is why we are told that the soul who eats and drinks unworthily eats and drinks condemnation to itself. But that judgement is not pronounced yet; it is when he comes again that he will pronounce judgement. It is then that he will say, " I never knew you ", or, " Come, ye blessed of my Father ". But, in his secret thoughts, we shall have been judged already. We are being judged, all the time.

XVII

I believe in the Holy Ghost (1)

I'VE ALWAYS been rather fond of the story, which I should think is almost certainly untrue, of a small boy in the East End of London who came to confession, and reduced his confession to the shortest possible limits by saying, " Bless me, Father, for I have sinned; thrown mud at buses and don't believe in the Holy Ghost ". I don't know what your experience may have been, but personally I have never been assailed by any temptation to throw mud at buses, and therefore I can't say what excuses the penitent may have had for this inconsiderate treatment of public property. But I think he was obviously a fool not to believe in the Holy Ghost. If you are going to believe in the Christian religion at all, and indeed in a sense if you are going to believe in any religion at all, I don't see how you can help believing in the Holy Ghost.

Suppose you come across one of those people, who are getting rather common in England nowadays, who don't quite like to describe themselves as Christians, but say they believe in God; yes, of course they believe in God. Suppose you try to pin them down, and find out what they really mean by it; suppose you ask, for example, " Do you believe that God is a Person, in the same sense as you and me? "—you will find that they reply, " Oh dear no; not a person; that would be anthropomorphism ". And you say, " Well, let's cut that part out; what do you really think God is like? How would you describe him? " And what's their answer? Why, that God is a Spirit, a sort of Force or Influence which manifests itself in various ways in and through this visible world of ours, but particularly manifests itself in the religious aspirations of human beings. To which you may very sensibly reply, " Oh, I see, you believe in the Holy Ghost, but not in the Father or the Son ".

Well, we believe in the Holy Ghost as well as the Father and the Son; and this afternoon we want to get some rough idea, at any rate, of what we mean by that. I think we are all rather apt, at the back of our minds, to forget that the Holy Spirit existed from all eternity, and to think of him as having come into existence on the Day of Pentecost. Well, of course that can't be true, because the Blessed Trinity has existed from all eternity, and it wouldn't be a Trinity without the Holy Spirit. So we've got to go right back, and think of God existing altogether outside time, independently of any worlds, or any angels for that matter. From all eternity there has been a multiplicity of life within the unity of the Godhead. God the Father, from all eternity, has spoken a Word; or if you prefer to put it in a rather more luminous way, from all eternity he has thought a thought of himself. When you or I think, the thought has no existence outside our own minds; but when the eternal Mind thinks of itself, it produces a Thought as eternal as itself, and that Thought is, like the eternal Mind, a Person. And so you get two persons within the Blessed Trinity, the eternal Mind and its eternal

Thought. And now, you can't imagine two Divine
Persons as existing side by side, can you, without
their having some relation to each other, some
attitude towards each other; and what that attitude
will be it is not difficult to guess; they will love one
another. And this Love, which springs at once from
the eternal Mind and its eternal Thought, binding
them to one another, is the Holy Spirit. That is why
we say that the Holy Spirit proceeds from the Father
and the Son. He is the conscious response of Love
which springs up between them; he goes out from
each of them to the other. That is not intended to be
an explanation of the doctrine of the Blessed Trinity,
because you cannot explain a mystery. But I think
that is as near as our minds will get to understanding
what the doctrine of the Trinity is about.

"Well," you say, "thank you very much; I expect
one ought to know about all that, but it seems rather
abstruse theology; now let's get on to Pentecost."
You're quite wrong again; we haven't nearly got on
to Pentecost yet. You didn't really think, did you,
that the Holy Spirit had nothing at all to do with the
visible creation until A.D. 30? If you did think that,
you were very badly out in your dates. Let's go back
to the second verse of the Bible, which tells us about
a time millions and millions of years ago. It says,
"the earth was void and empty, and darkness was
upon the face of the deep. And the Spirit of God
moved over the waters". The Hebrew for that is
even jollier; it says that the earth was all *tohu* and
bohu, which is a very good way of describing emptiness
and confusion. Try to imagine the earth, or the universe if you prefer it, without any light at all, just

undulations of matter, a great formless sea; no birds, no animals, no plants. And even then, " the Spirit of God moved over the waters ". As soon as there was any creation at all, even when it was all *tohu* and *bohu*, it gave out a kind of dumb response to its Creator; it was like a mist rising in a river valley at evening; and what was it? It was the Spirit of God.

When God created the universe, it was a sort of extension, you may say, of that eternal Thought of his, which we call his Word. That is why we always think of the Second Person of the Blessed Trinity as specially concerned in the work of creation. And as, within the Godhead itself, the answer to that act of Thought was an eternal Act of Love, the Holy Spirit; so, when God created things outside himself, there was an immediate response of love from his creatures; and that response was inspired in them by the Holy Spirit. And all through the Old Testament you get the idea of God's Spirit as pervading nature; " the Spirit of the Lord fills the whole world, and that which containeth all things hath knowledge of the Voice ".

What I'm saying just now isn't strict Catholic doctrine, all defined and printed in handbooks. But I think it's quite impossible to understand the Old Testament until you see that the Jews thought of the brute creation and even inanimate creation, mountains and valleys and sun and stars and beasts and birds and fishes—they always make a great point of the fishes—as conspiring to praise God all the time. And the medieval attitude was to accept that point of view about the response of creation to God, and to say, " Of course, that's the Holy Spirit; that's the response to God in nature. The Love which binds the Father and the Son overflows into created things, and makes them, too, aspire lovingly to God ".

But whether you value that idea about God in nature or not, it's quite certain that once *man* has come into being, the Holy Spirit has an office to perform here on earth. No, not on the Day of Pentecost; do stop being in such a hurry to get on to the Day of Pentecost. If you think the Holy Spirit never interfered in human affairs between the time of Adam and the time of St. Peter, you are a heretic. Because although this Creed we are having sermons about doesn't mention it, the longer creed which is said at Mass, the Nicene Creed, goes out of its way at this point to say, " who spoke by the prophets ". What does that mean? Well, in the first place what it says; it means that the Holy Spirit gave certain messages of warning to the Jews, by means of Isaias, Jeremy, Ezechiel, Daniel, Osee, Joel, Amos, Abdias, Jonas, Micheas, Nahum, Habacuc, Sophonias, Aggaeus, Zachary and Malachy. They were moved to say various things, many of which it is difficult to understand, and some of which they probably didn't understand themselves. They were carried away by the impetus of the Holy Spirit, and the great point is that many of the things which they said, or rather which he said through them, were prophecies about the coming of Jesus Christ. I don't suppose that Isaias quite knew what he was talking about when he said, " Behold, a Virgin shall conceive and bear a Son ". He just felt impelled, somehow, to say that, because that was what the Holy Spirit wanted him to say.

But, remember, this clause in the Nicene Creed means something more; it means that the *whole* of the Old Testament is inspired. And a lot of the books in the Old Testament are not prophecy exactly; they are pieces of history, and sometimes, like other pieces of history, it must be admitted, I think, that they are not very exciting to read, especially when you come across long lists of names. Well, all that is inspired. What do we mean when we say that it is inspired? Do we mean that the men who originally wrote those books, the books of Kings for example, simply sat down with a pen and took it all down as the Holy Spirit dictated it to them, just as you might take down a piece of dictation from one of the mistresses here? Must we picture them as saying, " Amasias was five and twenty years old when he began to reign (yes, I've got that), and he reigned nine and twenty years in Jerusalem (yes, I've got that), and his mother's name was Joadan (how do you spell Joadan, please?) " —and so on and so on? There have been people before now who have thought of the inspiration of Holy Scripture as if it were a mere process of dictation, of that kind.

But of course that is not the way in which the Old Testament was written, and you can prove it. Because if you look at the second book of Machabees (a thing which very few people do) you will find that the author describes to us how he wrote his book. He says that he has abridged in one book all the history that was written in five books by somebody called Jason of Cyrene. Now, there is no reason whatever to think that Jason of Cyrene was inspired. But the man—we don't know his name, or anything about him—who got to work and boiled down those five books into one book, the second book of Machabees, *was* inspired. And inspiration didn't make it an easy job, like dictation is; you know how when one is doing dictation one can be thinking about all sorts of jolly things at the same time, and do it more or less automatically. But no, this man says, " As to ourselves indeed, in undertaking this work of abridging, we have taken in hand no easy task; yea, rather a business full of watching and sweat." It was like writing an essay, when you have to get the stuff out of books but put it down in your own words. And when he had finished, although it was an inspired book, this man wasn't in the least certain that it would be a best seller. He says at the end, " I will here make an end of my narration, which if I have done well, and as becometh the history, it is what I desired; but if not so perfectly, it must be pardoned me ". Just what you feel inclined to say when you've finished writing an essay. He sat down and wrote quite an ordinary book, in quite an ordinary way; and yet it was inspired.

What do we mean when we say that it was inspired, or that any book of the Old Testament was inspired? Not that it was *dictated* by the Holy Spirit, but that the Holy Spirit helped the writers, watched over the process and saw they did it right; put ideas, perhaps, into their heads, which made them say, " That's rather a good idea; I never thought of that before "— but it all seemed to come out of their heads, and indeed it *did* come out of their heads; because the Holy Spirit works in our heads. That doesn't necessarily mean that every word in the Old Testament, taken

quite literally, is infallibly accurate. You find it stated
in the Psalms, for instance, that God has made the
round world so sure that it cannot be moved. And
when Galileo, or rather, first Copernicus and then
Galileo, produced the idea which we all believe in
nowadays, that the earth travels round and round on
its own axis; that the sun doesn't really " set ", all
that happens is that we have lost sight of it because
we've turned round the corner—when that idea was
produced, a lot of people, chiefly Protestants, said,
" That's heresy! The Bible tells us that the earth
can't be moved, and here are these people wanting us
to believe that it's speeding round and round like
mad! " But of course that was idiotic of them. The
Psalms weren't written to teach us lessons in geo-
graphy; they were poetry, and the person who wrote
that verse was just talking in the ordinary language
of his time. So you can't be certain that every word
of the Old Testament is *literally* true. But you can be
certain that the theology of the Old Testament, once
you have understood it properly and made allowances
for the Hebrew way of saying things, *must* be true;
because when it was written the Holy Spirit was at
work to see that the thing got done right.

And, remember, the Holy Spirit wasn't at work
only amongst the Jews. All through those centuries
before our Lord came, whenever a human heart
aspired to God, it was the same old story; it was the
Third Person of the Blessed Trinity carrying out in
this visible, created world the same work which he
carries out in the uncreated, invisible world of
eternity. He was making, in us, that response of love
towards the eternal Father which it is his nature to

make. In spite of the Fall, there's a kind of instinct which makes man look up to God, try to get back to God, and that instinct is the silent working of the Holy Spirit, in the very heart even of unredeemed mankind.

There, now, we haven't got on to the Day of Pentecost after all; that's what comes of interrupting. But all this that I've been saying to you isn't really waste of time, because it's very difficult to get a right idea about the work of the Holy Spirit in the order of grace, until you've got some idea of what the Holy Spirit does in the order of nature. His essential office is to be the response of love in our hearts to the goodness of God.

XVIII

I believe in the Holy Ghost (2)

THIS SUNDAY, we really must get on to the Day of Pentecost. Try and imagine the picture of it; Jerusalem, quite a small town, with very narrow streets at that, crowded with thousands of Jewish pilgrims from all over the known world. They had come there to celebrate the Feast of Weeks, which was the Jewish harvest festival; because in that part of the world you get the wheat harvest in by Whit Sunday, and that must give you a nice long slack interval before the potatoes want picking. All these visitors from the parts of Libya about Cyrene—the General Montgomery country—and Elam, which would be right down somewhere in Iraq, and Pontus, not far from the southern end of where the Russians were fighting the Germans; nearly all Jews, but born and bred in a foreign country, so that they were familiar with the odd dialects the country people used in all these outlying parts of the world; Greek would be their natural language, but they'd have to know the local dialect so as to be able to talk to the people who came in to do business with them. I don't know if you've ever been to Lourdes, but I should think it must have been very much like Lourdes at the height of the pilgrimage season.

And what were they doing there, all these people? Were they really very much interested in thanking

God for the harvest having been got in in one rather unimportant district of the province of Syria? No, but it was the tradition to rally round when the great feasts came on in Jerusalem; their fathers had always done it, and they weren't going to give it up; they were devout men, and it was the thing to do. But it must have seemed rather pointless, rather out of the world-picture, now that Judaea had become such a very unimportant place, and was ruled by foreign conquerors. So they drifted about the streets, a great tide of humanity, without any vital religious inspiration to rally them. It was rather like that tide of undifferentiated matter we were talking about last Sunday, the *tohu* and *bohu* which were the first result of God's creation. Was it possible that the Spirit of God would move on these sluggish waters, too?

And of course, quite suddenly, it did. Quite suddenly, here and there in the crowd, you saw the extraordinary sight of a working man from Galilee making his way to the temple, shouting out God's praises in an uncontrollable way that made you wonder whether he was drunk, though you had only just cleared away breakfast. And when you got nearer, you found that it was St. Peter shouting out phrases in the language of Cappadocia, or St. Thomas talking fluent Parthian, or St. Matthew giving you bits of his Gospel in the Berber dialect of Northern Africa. And the infection of their example spread; people took up their cries, hardly knowing what they were doing, in a babel of strange tongues; from that *tohu* and *bohu* of nationalities the response of the Holy Spirit went up once more in aspirations of love

towards the God who had made all nations to dwell
on the face of the earth.

What did it mean? Well, it meant in general that,
this day, the Catholic Church was born. But we shall
have to talk about the Catholic Church, I suppose,
about the end of September, so I won't enlarge on
that subject just now. The Holy Spirit does dwell in
the Catholic Church as a whole, inspires its official
teachings infallibly, makes its doctors and theologians
hit the right nail on the head more often than not, and
prevents popes and bishops, anyhow, from making the
wrong move in practical politics all the time. But I
want to think more particularly this afternoon of the
inspiration of the Holy Spirit as it affects the life of the
individual Christian, as it affects you and me.

The first people to receive the Holy Spirit were, as
we have seen, the Apostles. And they needed his
inspiration for a special reason; they were going out
all over the world to preach Jesus Christ, and they
were going to make themselves unpopular, because
they would come up against a lot of vested interests
in doing so. They would be brought to trial before
rulers and magistrates, who would enquire rather
unintelligently, as rulers and magistrates do, " Here,
what's all this? " And what were they going to say?
Our Lord himself warned them about that, if you
remember; he told them, " Don't bother about what
you are going to say. When the time comes, it won't
be you that speak, it will be the spirit of your
Heavenly Father that speaks in you ". That was the
immediate office of the Holy Spirit, when he came to
earth on the Day of Pentecost to begin a new dis-
pensation; he was to enable the Apostles to put up

an inspired defence when they were brought to trial in courts of law. And that is why our Lord promised them that he would send them a Paraclete. In the Protestant translation of the Bible that word is translated, " the Comforter "; but that, I'm afraid, was a howler made by the Protestant translators of the Bible; they mixed up the active with the passive, the sort of thing I am sure any of you would scorn to do. No, the Paraclete, a long and ugly word which you have come across before now in hymns, means primarily the lawyer who defends you in a court of justice; he has to explain that you did really mean to pay for the six yards of silk you took off the counter, and if you were found leaving the shop with the silk hidden in your umbrella, that was just absentmindedness. The Advocate, that is the primary meaning of Paraclete; though I don't think it makes a very pretty translation, because it suggests a rather prosy old gentleman, and a Scot at that.

But it goes deeper, of course. The Friend in Need— that is really what is meant by the word Paraclete. And you will find in St. Paul's writings that he didn't merely think of the Holy Spirit as suggesting to us useful things to say in a court of law; he makes suggestions to us about our prayers. " The Spirit," he says, " helps our weakness; we don't know how to pray as we ought to, but the Spirit himself makes petitions on our behalf, with groanings which cannot be uttered." So, you see, we don't have to think of the assistance of the Holy Spirit as something which we need when it is necessary for us to talk in public; like the Scots minister who began an extempore speech by saying, " When I'm called upon suddenly like this,

I just say what the Holy Spirit puts into my mind; but if you give me an hour or two for preparation, I can do much better ". The assistance of the Holy Spirit is something which we want every time we say our prayers; indeed, I suppose if you look at the thing properly the right way to put it is that every time we say our prayers it is the Holy Spirit who is praying *in* us.

What makes it difficult for us to realize that, is that we don't distinguish as carefully as we ought to between the extraordinary and the ordinary operations of the Holy Spirit. Except when the Holy Spirit makes his presence felt by outward manifestations, we forget that he's there. You see, when you were confirmed you received exactly the same gift which our Lady and the Apostles received on the Day of Pentecost. But you didn't thereupon get up and start praising God in Tamil or Choctaw; why was that? Because the Holy Spirit doesn't, as a rule, signalize his coming by these strange outward manifestations; he only does it occasionally, where it is specially important to call attention to what is happening. It's the same, after all, when you read the lives of the Saints. You read about Saints who went off into an ecstasy for five or six hours at a time, when they were saying their prayers, quite unconscious of what was going on around them. When that sort of thing happens, you can see at once that the Holy Spirit is taking a hand in it. But when *you* are kneeling there just going on saying, " Holy Mary, Mother of God, pray for us sinners now and at the hour of our death ", you don't think of the Holy Spirit as having anything to do with *that*; it's just *you* trying to say your prayers, and not making much of it even so.

What we ought to try and realize much more than we do is that these very second-rate prayers of ours are really prayed in us, so far as they are prayers at all, by the Holy Spirit. No doubt our minds are in a rather confused state, full of distractions; there's a good deal of *tohu* and *bohu* about it. But the same echo of Divine Love which awoke in that formless creation, when the Spirit of God moved upon the face of the waters, awakes in you when you pray; the wind of Pentecost is blowing through the world still, and you are like a reed rustling in the wind; the motion, the activity, is his really, not yours; or rather, your activity conspires with his. And I think we sometimes make a mistake about that when our prayers aren't going too well. We try to make a tremendous effort at concentration, try to pump up more energy from somewhere inside ourselves, and reduce ourselves to a better state of prayer by sheer will-power. Whereas I think really the right attitude for us is to fall back more on the Holy Spirit, and leave things more to him. To say, " Go on praying in me, Holy Spirit; I can't do anything, I know I can't do anything, by these frantic efforts of my own. Every time I really try to settle down to it I find myself thinking about the holidays, or about that girl I've quarrelled with, and nothing seems to come. But I *know* it's all right really, because it is *you* who do the praying; I am only a dumb instrument for you to make noises with. Since I find my own efforts make so little difference, let me keep still and leave room for you to go on praying, praying in me ".

And it's the same with the inspirations of the Holy Spirit, with the guidance which he gives us. We all ought to pray to the Holy Spirit for guidance much more than we do. The reason, partly, why we don't do it more is that we expect too much of him, and therefore we are disappointed. When we ask the Holy Spirit to show us what we ought to do on this occasion or that, we expect that a sudden, miraculous illumination will come into our minds; that we shall be told, as if by a voice speaking in our ears, what we ought to do. We have read about that kind of thing in the lives of the Saints, about St. Joan of Arc being told by her voices that she must go and tell the King of France to get himself crowned, and St. Catherine of Siena being suddenly inspired to tell the Pope to go back to Rome, and so on. Well, here again it's quite true that the Holy Spirit can, and sometimes does, give very holy people unexpected, miraculous guidance of this kind; it just comes to them—you can't imagine it as being the result of any human calculations of their own.

Sometimes, indeed, it hardly seems to make sense. There was St. Alexius, whose feast we kept yesterday. He left his home as a young man on a pilgrimage, and only came back years later, when they didn't recognize him. But they were good people, St. Alexius's parents, and they took pity on this rather half-witted, very holy young man who had dropped in on them, and let him stay in the house. So he lived in his father's house for seventeen years, without letting on who he was, and it was only found out by a written message which he left behind him when he died. The collect for yesterday asks God that as we celebrate St.

Alexius's feast, so we may follow his example; but of course if we all did it would create a great deal of confusion and make our parents very unhappy. No, that was a special vocation which the Holy Spirit had for St. Alexius; and he put the idea into St. Alexius's head by a special, miraculous inspiration. But you and I mustn't expect that kind of thing.

We mustn't expect that kind of thing; but we must pray to the Holy Spirit for his guidance, all the same. Suppose you're leaving school, and can't make up your mind whether to apply for the Army or the Navy or the Air Force. It's perfectly reasonable to keep a novena to the Holy Spirit and ask for his guidance about it; but you mustn't expect to have a vision of your patron saint dressed in a sky-blue uniform, or something of that kind, so as to make it quite certain what it is God wants you to do. No, you keep your novena, and at the same time you take advice from your relations and friends, and you try to balance up in your own mind the arguments for and against this or that course. And when you have made up your mind in this way, you know that, if you kept your novena faithfully, the Holy Spirit *has* helped you to make up your mind, although there is nothing to show for it. Probably, sooner or later, you will come across a queer kind of Protestants who talk a great deal about " guidance ", and think you ought never to do anything, not even cross the street or buy a new hat, unless you get a sudden, unaccountable indication that it is God's will for you to do so. They won't believe that if you've made up your mind to do a thing as the result of human calculations, the Holy Spirit can have had anything to do with it. And that, you see, is want of faith on their part. They imagine that the Holy Spirit can never interfere in the course of human affairs without making a splash about it and producing a kind of miraculous certainty in people's minds about what they ought to do. They can't believe that he has ordinary, as well as extraordinary, operations.

The primary office of the Holy Spirit is not to create a nine days' wonder by appearing suddenly in rushing winds, and tongues of fire. He is the eternal Love that proceeds from the Father and the Divine Word, producing in human creatures and on behalf of human creatures, without their knowing it, a response of love to the Divine Love which created them.

XIX

I believe in the holy Catholic Church (1)

SOMEBODY, I forget who, in talking about the art of writing, said, " The adjective is the enemy of the noun ". I expect that sounds pretty good nonsense to you, as if I had said, " The butter is the enemy of the bread ". Well, whether you can have too much butter on your bread is a matter of opinion, but I think it is pretty certain that, in writing, you spoil the effect of your noun by piling up adjectives round it, and that is the meaning of the phrase I have just quoted to you. If that is true, we Catholics have got hold of a very bad literary tradition. We are always tacking on unnecessary adjectives. We don't talk about " God ", we talk about " Almighty God ", as if we should be idiotic enough to forget that God is Almighty unless we continually reminded ourselves of the fact. Catholic tradespeople sending out circulars always are careful to explain that they are ready to supply the reverend clergy with bicycle-clips or cork-screws or whatever it may be—why not just call them " the clergy "? And I expect you have come across people in the holidays who refer to the community here as " the good nuns "; what's the use of pointing that out? Of course nuns are good; that's what they are there for. Now when we refer in the *Credo* to the *holy* Catholic Church, is that word holy just an

unnecessary flourish put in out of politeness, like
" Almighty " and " reverend " and " good "? Or
does it really *tell* us something; is it something *extra*
that the *Credo* pledges us to believe in?

Well, the answer to that is that the word " holy "
isn't just put in for fun; the *Credo* doesn't waste words.
The holiness of the Church is something you and I
have got to believe in; and it isn't, after all, so obvious
as you might suppose. When St. Paul, as I was
telling you the Sunday before last, talks about the
Church as the Bride of Christ, he tells us that
our Lord wants to present it before himself " not
having spot or wrinkle or any such thing ". That
glorious bride whom he means to unite to himself, in
heaven, is the perfect Church, the total body of
souls who are to be redeemed and are to enjoy everlasting life in heaven. But that, if you come to think
of it, is not the Church as we know it, and for two
reasons.

In the first place, being a Catholic doesn't necessarily mean that you will go to heaven. It would be
all right if it did, wouldn't it? It would save us all
a lot of trouble and anxiety. No, the Church as we
know it, the Church on earth, is a very mixed lot.
That's an idea which Protestants often find it difficult
to understand. I remember long ago saying in a
sermon that it's probably safer to leave your umbrella
at the door of a Wesleyan chapel than to leave it at
the door of a Catholic church. Every now and then
I hear of that remark being quoted with great satisfaction by Wesleyans. But I don't think they quite
got my point; my point was that the Catholic Church
is a mixed lot, and that proves that it is the Church

which our Lord Jesus Christ came to found. Because he told us, quite unmistakably, that his Church on earth *would* be a mixed lot.

That is the point of the parable about the farmer who sowed good seed in his field, and then somebody who didn't like him came along at night and sowed cockle on the top of it, so that the whole thing was a glorious mess. And you'll remember that the farm servants, while the crop was still young, asked the farmer whether they should settle down to weed it; but the farmer said, " No; that would be waste of a lot of time; the thing to do is to wait till the harvest, gather all the crop together, and sort it out afterwards ". I don't know whether that would be considered good farming nowadays; but that is evidently what they would have done in our Lord's time. And it is the same, our Lord says, with the kingdom of heaven—by which, as usual, he means his Church. Bad Christians and good Christians will go on side by side till the harvest; bad Christians going to church with the good Christians, and getting buried in the same church-yard as the good Christians, but it doesn't mean they'll go to heaven with the good Christians. And there's another parable of the same kind, about a net let down into the sea and enclosing all kinds of different fish, some fit to eat, some not. What did the fishermen do? Drop the net and say, " What's the use of loading up with all these dog-fish and conger-eels? " No, they pulled the whole lot in to shore, and sorted them out when they got there. And that, our Lord tells us, is what the angels do. The net is the Church; it contains all sorts; it's only on the other side of death, when we meet our judgement, that the mess will be tidied up. Our Church is the Church of Judas Iscariot.

That's one reason why the Church as we know it is not the same as that perfect Church which our Lord will espouse to himself in heaven. There is another reason, and a more cheering one. There are some Catholics who will not go to heaven; but, to make up, there are some people who will go to heaven although they are not Catholics. They are not Catholics, because they were brought up, say, as Protestants, and nothing has ever happened to make them see that they ought to be Catholics. Their minds are prejudiced against the Church from the start, and the Catholics they happen to have come across weren't the kind of Catholics who did much good. So these people went on as Protestants, being religious according to their lights, being sorry for it when they sinned, trusting in our Lord to save them when they lay on their death-beds. Those people are going to heaven; they remained outside the Church through what we call " invincible ignorance ". That doesn't mean they were very stupid people; many of them are not. It means that they couldn't have been expected, with the chances at their disposal, to find out that the Catholic Church is the means by which our Lord wants mankind to be saved.

There you are, then; the Church of Christ on earth isn't exactly the same lot of people that will be Christ's Church in heaven. Christ's Church in heaven will be a hundred per cent saved; Christ's Church on earth, if we may use what is more or less his own metaphor, is a mixed bag. And yet it is of this mixed bag that we say, " I believe the Catholic Church to be holy ". Judas betrays his Master—Judas, the Catholic; and we still say, " The Church is holy ". Cardinals poison one another, in the history books we read, and we still say, " The Church is holy ". We go to Mass at Farm Street, and there's such a pious-looking man saying his rosary just behind us, and when we come back from making our Communion the pious-looking man has disappeared, and our bag has disappeared, too, and we still say, " The Church is holy ". What is it that leaves our faith quite undisturbed after all these uncomfortable incidents?

It's worth mentioning that point, because it is a point which is constantly coming up in argument. Even if it were possible for our Protestant friends to say, " You call your Church holy; but I don't see that you are any better than other people ", it would be bad enough. But it's worse than that—our Protestant friends have generally got the impression that we are *worse* than other people. And it is extraordinary, if you follow the reports of criminal trials in the newspapers, what a lot of Joseph Antonies and Patrick Aloysiuses seem to figure in the murder cases, or at any rate to have both feet in the black market. There's a story of some visitor who went to see the Catholic chaplain at Sing-Sing, which is the big State prison in the United States. And this chaplain was saying what unscrupulous stories Protestants were always inventing to discredit the Church. " For instance," he said, " you'll often be told that all the prisoners who are executed here are Catholics. Well, there are five prisoners now waiting for the electric chair, and one of them's a Jew."

I say it's worth mentioning that point, but we really haven't time to go into it. There is a lot to be said about it; about how Catholics in England are mostly poor, for example, and it's mostly poor people, in England, who get sent to prison; and how Catholic names are easier to recognize, so that one notices the Catholics more. But what's more to our immediate purpose is to remind ourselves that the Church does produce sanctity. When people think of bad popes, the first name that comes into their heads is Pope Alexander the Sixth. Do you remember what his surname was? Borgia. And if you look up your Missal you will find that today's feast is the feast of St. Francis—Borgia. Same family, you see, but a different type. St. Francis Borgia, even before he entered the Society of Jesus, used to make a five hours' meditation first thing every morning, and that takes some doing. So far from administering poison to other people, St. Francis's efforts seem to have been largely directed to making his own food taste nasty. When he had to take a pill he always sucked it; not because he couldn't make it go down, but because he thought it would be a good punishment for his sins; he was very strong on his sins, though nobody else could quite make out what they were. The cook put wormwood in the soup one day, by mistake, and St. Francis didn't rush down the passage shouting, " Where's that cook? "—he thanked the cook and said, " God bless you, you are the only person who seems to understand the kind of food that really suits me ". All that sort of thing you may find now and then, here and there, in the lives of other people; but there's a quality about the lives of the Catholic Saints in general which I don't think you do find elsewhere; a kind of gracious fanaticism. And it isn't only the things the Saints do, of course, it's the things God does through his Saints; the miracles, the ecstasies—all that is the holiness of the Church coming out, all through the centuries, just as in the days of the Apostles.

And there's another thing about the Church which makes it easy to recognize her holiness—the existence of the religious orders. People all over the world, in enormous numbers, getting up at unearthly hours in the morning and spending all that time in church and dressing so uncomfortably and not going to the cinema, and working so hard for nothing, looking after you and teaching you and picking your hair-brushes out of the lavender when you throw them out of the front window—all that great conspiracy of people living an ordered life and a life of much self-denial for the love of God. I don't mean that you get nothing like that outside the Church, but you get nothing on that scale among the other forms of Christianity; and that's why we say that the existence of the religious orders is a permanent witness to, a permanent expression of, the holiness of the Church.

But of course when we call the Church holy we don't simply mean that it is a collection of holy people. To suppose that a member of a holy Church is *necessarily* a holy person is to be guilty of a fallacy which is called, in logic, the fallacy of division. Suppose, for example, you were to argue in this way: " The sun never sets on the British Empire; I am a citizen of the British Empire; therefore the sun never sets on me "—that would be idiotic. Because the thing is true of a set of people taken as a whole, you can't necessarily assume that it is true of each one of them taken separately. And I think it is a really startling difference between the Catholic Church and any other Christian denomination, that other Christians think it is up to *them* to be holy in order to bring up the average of holiness, so to speak, in their particular denomination; but we Catholics have a quite different instinct—we think of the Church as a holy thing, whether we are holy or not. We expect it to make us holy; we don't imagine it to be our job to make it holy. We don't feel like people pushing a hand-cart, and keeping it going through their own exertions; we feel like people hanging on behind a cart, using our legs, to be sure, but getting the cart to do all the work for us. It's quite natural to us, for instance, to think of it as " Mother Church "; but I don't think anybody belonging to the Salvation Army would ever call it " Mother Army ". It is a reservoir, a power-house of holiness, this Church of ours; not a mere collection of holy people.

When we have said that, I think it's perhaps as well to remind ourselves that if we want to impress people outside with the holiness of the Church there is only one way to do it, and that is to be holy. By which I don't simply mean that we should try, if possible, to keep out of prison. I mean that we should be really generous in our love of God, really honest in our ambition to follow Jesus Christ. What holds up the conversion of England, I always think, is not so much the wickedness of a few Catholics, as the dreadful ordinariness of most Catholics. There is a temptation for us, simply because we belong to a holy Church, just to sit back and be passengers, and say, " I'm not going to bother about being anything above the average; I leave the Church to do the holiness for me ". But we have got to match the Church, you and I, to wear her colours. And when we say, " I believe in the holy Catholic Church ", we mean, among other things, " I believe that holiness is a good thing; that holiness would be a good thing for me ".

XX

I believe in the holy Catholic Church (2)

PERHAPS I ought to explain, for the benefit of some people here who have only just joined up, that this sermon is one of a course of sermons about the *Credo*. It's been going on and on and on, term after term, and no amount of coughing or shuffling is going to prevent me finishing it. I'm afraid that those of you who have just come may feel rather annoyed at coming in in the middle like this—it's rather like those serial stories in the newspapers which tell you to look out for another thrilling instalment next week. I'm afraid I can't give you a synopsis of the previous chapters, because it would take up too much time. Only, if you did have to come in in the middle—and it was your own fault, you see, for not coming to school earlier—let's be glad that you chipped in where you did, at a really important article of the Creed like this.

You see, when you say, " I believe in the holy Catholic Church ", you've said a mouthful. I shouldn't wonder if it takes us most of the present term to get through it, especially if you will keep on butting in with objections. If you believe in the holy Catholic Church, then it follows that you believe in all the rest of the *Credo*; it would be silly to believe in the Church and not believe in what the Church tells you. So we'll get right down to it; and just for this

Sunday I don't think we'll worry about the Church being holy or the Church being Catholic; we'll just stick to the idea of the Church in general, and remind ourselves what the word Church means, and how jolly it is to have a Church to belong to.

If you look up the word Church in a really large dictionary, it will tell you several things about it; such as that there are really twenty different ways of spelling it, which is good news for those of us who aren't very handy at dictation, and that it is connected by derivation with various words in other languages, for instance with the Old Slavonic word CRIKY. But what nobody seems to know is what it is derived from. However, that doesn't matter much, because it is used to translate the Greek word, which is also a Latin word, *ecclesia*. And *ecclesia* means a collection of people specially appointed for a purpose. In ancient Athens, for example, they called their House of Commons the *ecclesia*, the national assembly. And when Almighty God brought the children of Israel out of Egypt, he called them his *ecclesia*, his assembly. They were to be his representatives, in a world which had gone idolatrous. He had called them out (that is the root meaning of the word) from Egypt, from a land given up to the most extraordinary superstitions, a land where people used to worship crocodiles and cats. He had called them out into the desert of Sinai, where there were no crocodiles or cats to worship. They were to be his chosen people, his assembly, his picked lot. And that was the word which our Lord took over, that was the idea which our Lord took over when he came to earth and founded what we call his Church. When he said to St. Peter, " You are my Rock, and

I am going to build my Church on this Rock ", he was setting out to do the same thing which God had done when he called his people out of Egypt. Moses had started a Church, the Church of Israel; now our Lord was going to start a Church of his own—that is what he meant by " my Church ". He, too, was going to have a picked lot of people to serve him and to represent him, and that picked lot was you and me.

Part of the fun of being a Christian is belonging to a Church. It gives you a sort of cosy feeling, doesn't it, to be one of a picked lot. You know what it's like, when you're playing some game in which it's necessary to pick sides; there you all are in a crowd, perhaps twenty of you, and then the captain of one side says, " I'll have you, and you, and you ", and all at once you begin to have a friendly sort of feeling for the other people on *your* side, even if you only know them quite slightly; they are your comrades now, although they were only comparative strangers to you two minutes ago. That feeling of comradeship, of belonging to the same crowd, is for some reason one of the delights of the human mind. That is why people become Freemasons, and hold secret meetings and dress up in curious aprons and invent pass-words and signs and so on; it gives them a sense of comradeship. When you shake hands, I'm told, if you think the other person is a Freemason you give him a special grip, and he gives you a special grip in return, and then you are both frightfully bucked, because you feel you've met a friend. Perhaps that doesn't appeal to you very much, because after all Catholics aren't allowed to be Freemasons; and for that matter women aren't allowed to be Freemasons, which some people think is the reason why the Freemason secret has been kept so well. But it's the same really with any kind of organization you belong to; the girl guides, for instance. Of course I've never been a girl guide, and if it comes to that I was never a boy scout; because if the terrible truth must be told the boy scouts hadn't been invented when I was a boy. But I imagine that if you are a guide, and come across another girl in the holidays who tells you she is a guide, too, it gives you a sort of cosy feeling; you have something in common with her, you belong to the same crowd. It's a natural human instinct to get together and form associations like that.

For Christian people, and for us Catholics especially, this feeling of comradeship forms part of the stuff of our religion. It gives us a curious lightening of the heart, difficult rather to explain, when we find out suddenly that the policeman who stands on duty at the street corner or the girl who does our hair or the man who comes in to wind up the clocks is a Catholic, too. And by the time it's possible to go travelling again, you'll find something of the same kind, I think, about visiting Catholic countries. You get an added enjoyment out of it from the mere feeling that all these strange people, talking a quite unintelligible language and dressing in rather bad taste and driving their cars on the wrong side of the road, are, neverthe-less, Catholics—there is a bond, after all, between you and them. When our Lord Jesus Christ came down to earth he became MAN, he understood, and he allowed for, all our human instincts, even our quite unreasonable human instincts. And he allowed for this human instinct of comradeship by founding a

Church. He went round, like the captain of a side, saying, " I'll have you and you and you "; and all at once we, the people on whom his choice fell, became friendly with one another; we all belong to the same crowd, a very big crowd and a very mixed crowd, but all of us vaguely united in our sympathies because we all belong to him.

It's true, he didn't often talk about his Church. Not, I mean, under that name; usually he called it the kingdom of God, or the kingdom of heaven. Nine times out of ten when our Lord uses either of those phrases he is really talking about his Church. But we needn't stop just now to consider why he did that. The person who really put the word " Church " on the map was St. Paul. I think if you count up you will find that the word " Church " occurs about sixty times in his writings, which aren't after all very long. It's true that he sometimes confuses us by talking about the Church at Ephesus or the Church at Philippi as if they were two quite different things, like the Church of England and the Church of Scotland. But he doesn't mean that. You see, he is quite ready to talk about " the Church " in so and so's household. He would have talked about us as " the Church at Aldenham ". To him, the Church was part of the air he breathed, and just as you can talk about the air of Brighton or the air of Blackpool, but it's all the same air really, so he would talk about the Church here and the Church there, but to him it was all one thing; one great, glorious association, called out, and called together, by the word of Jesus Christ.

But, of course, it isn't just an association, like the girl guides, which is meant to make us nicer and more self-respecting people, who remember to brush our teeth and salute the Flag. The Church is a supernatural association, which is meant to get us to heaven. It isn't merely something which unites us together, you and me, it is the thing which unites us to Jesus Christ. And that, I think you can say, is the main difference between the Protestant and the Catholic idea of salvation. The Protestant hopes to be saved just by faith in Jesus Christ; the Catholic hopes to be saved by living and dying as a member of the Church which Jesus Christ founded. You can put it quite simply in this way. If you think of the human race as sailors, travelling over a sea, which is this sinful world, and trying to reach a harbour, which is heaven—the Protestant thinks of getting to heaven as something like being washed up to shore as a ship-wrecked man, clinging to an empty barrel. But the Catholic thinks of salvation as sailing into port on a ship, and that ship is the Church of Jesus Christ.

St. Paul doesn't use that metaphor, although St. Peter does. St. Paul has three favourite metaphors by which he tries to give us some idea of what the Church is and what it ought to mean to us. He is always referring to it either as the bride of Christ, or as the temple of Christ, or as the body of Christ. Let's just go through those three metaphors, and see what he means by them.

The bride of Jesus Christ—you all know how, in the fairy-stories, the prince is never allowed to marry the princess until he has killed at least one dragon and an assortment of giants, and probably fetched a jug of water from the well at the world's end, or done something energetic like that. He has to work hard, has the prince, to win his princess. And although things aren't *quite* like that in real life, they are *rather* like that in real life. A man can't reasonably expect a woman to marry him until he has got a job, so as to be able to support her. And, while I shouldn't advise you, later on, to marry anybody for his money, I shouldn't advise you, either, to get engaged to a man who hopes that if he practises a bit more he may get taken on as a saxophone in a dance-band—you'll find your father will kick like a mule if you do that, and quite rightly. A man has got to win his bride; and so St. Paul thinks of our Lord as coming to earth to work and to win a bride for himself, and that bride is the Church. So that the love of Christ for his Church, the love of the Church for Christ, is something as strong, as lasting, as unselfish, as consuming, as the love of a man for a woman, of a woman for a man. He can't talk about husbands and wives without going off into a long digression about Christ and his Church —that was the way St. Paul saw it. You and I, then, if we want to win the love of Christ, have got to be loyal first and foremost to his Church; it is as part of that Church that he sees your soul and mine, as part of that Church that he wants to win it for himself.

And then, suddenly switching off, St. Paul will begin talking about the Church as a great building, about you and me as stones set in that building. " You are fellow-citizens of the saints," he tells us, " built upon the foundation of the apostles and prophets, Jesus Christ himself being the chief corner-stone. Each of us is fitted in, wedged in, into his proper place in this building,. and the whole of it rests, ultimately, on Jesus Christ." And that is meant to show how important unity is in the Church, and how we all depend on one another. You know how sometimes people tell you that such and such a thing isn't very edifying. If I were to come in to Mass every morning five minutes late and tying up the strings of the chasuble as I went, people would say it wasn't very edifying. What does that word mean, edifying? Why, simply building up. You and I are building up one another's faith all the time, like stones in a building wedged together so that one stone keeps another in place. I dare say you feel rather wedged together, because there are rather a lot of you this term, and you look a bit like a tin of sardines. If one of you were to faint now, she would probably knock her next-door neighbour down as well as herself. And that's what the Church is like; we are all supporting one another, depending on one another; and your faith, however unimportant a Catholic you are, is valuable to Jesus Christ because it is helping, in its small way, to shore up that vast edifice, his Church.

But after all stones are dead things, and buildings are dead things; so St. Paul likes to be even more daring than that. Instead of telling us that we are a building of which Christ is the corner stone, he will tell us that we are a body, of which Christ is the head. If you cut off a person's head, that person dies; the brain is the centre of that nerve-system by which we live. So Christ, as our Head, gives life to his Church; it is from him that the graces which we need flow into every part of the body, flow into you and me. When you have a pain in your big toe, you don't really feel it in your big toe, you feel it in your brain. So closely is the whole system of the human body knit together;

and you and I as members of Christ, as limbs of Christ, are bound together as closely, as really with him as a human body is bound together, and bound up with its head.

I thought it better to get through these general considerations about the Church first of all, because if you come to think of it this doctrine of the Church, this notion of getting in touch with God only as part of an institution, is so very much a Christian and a Catholic idea; you don't get it in other religions; Buddhists and Mohammedans don't get this cosy feeling we Catholics have of all belonging together, all being part of one thing. And then we'll go on next Sunday to talk about the CATHOLIC Church, and what being a Catholic means and ought to mean

XXI

I believe in the holy Catholic Church (3)

WE TALKED last Sunday about what a Church was and
what was the point of believing in it, and the fun of
believing in it. Let's remember, this Sunday, that it's
got to be the *Catholic* Church. And let's get the
meaning of the word clear first. If you say that a
thing is catholic you mean that it is all over the place.
It's like Woolworth's; you can find a Woolworth's if
you go into Birmingham, or Wolverhampton, or
Shrewsbury, but you won't find a Little & Cooper
in Birmingham or Wolverhampton or Shrewsbury,
you have to go to Bridgnorth to find Little & Cooper.
And Woolworth is the same sort of thing everywhere;
it sells you the same kind of goods—whether it is a
good kind of goods is a different question, but that
doesn't concern us here. You know what to expect
of it—that is the point. It's all over the place, all over
the big towns of England; and the Catholic Church is
all over the world.

I'm only labouring this point because you will sometimes find the word catholic, spelt with a small C, used
in a rather different sense. You may read in an
obituary notice in the newspaper, for example, that
the deceased gentleman's tastes were catholic. That
means that he liked a lot of different things; he preferred whisky, perhaps, but he was quite happy with

beer if he couldn't get it, and if the rain prevented him getting his game of golf he was quite happy going to the pictures instead—he didn't *mind*. And some rather stupid people talk as if the Catholic Church ought to be something like that, a Church which doesn't *mind*. It ought to include everybody, it ought to be everybody's cup of tea. If there are people who want to get divorced, then the Catholic Church ought to let them get divorced; if there are people who don't believe in hell, then it oughtn't to bother about believing in hell. A really Catholic Church, they say, would include everybody, even the people who don't believe in hell, even the people who insist on getting divorced. A Church can't really be Catholic unless it's what they call broad-minded—that's what they think. But, as we've seen, Catholic doesn't mean that; it means *existing all over the world*.

And at the same time, remember, it's got to be *the same* all over the world; there would be no point in its existing everywhere if it taught one set of doctrines in England and another in Portugal, had one set of rules in Switzerland and another in Madagascar. Of course, that doesn't extend down to the tiniest details of dress and behaviour; Catholic priests wear beards, for example, in missionary countries, but they don't in England, except the Capuchins. And there are bigger differences than that you would come across if you were in a position to travel about the world; there are parts of the world, for example, in which Mass isn't said in Latin, but in other languages still more old-fashioned and still more incomprehensible. But in general, that is, in all matters of importance, the Catholic Church is the same all over the world. It

unites different nations, different races, in a *common*
creed; that is the point of its being Catholic.

I was telling you last Sunday, only you've forgotten,
that the word *ecclesia*, Church, was originally applied
to the congregation or assembly of the Jewish people;
they liked to think of themselves as God's Church.
And so indeed they were, they were all the Church
God had then. But they were not his Catholic
Church, and they didn't pretend to be. They were
scattered far and wide, especially after the time of
their captivity in Babylon; but they were still a
nation, and their church was the church of their own
nation—they didn't want outsiders to join it, or anyhow, not much. The Jewish idea of God and his
Church was that of a family affair. Our Lord Jesus
Christ changed all that; he chose out, almost from the
first, Gentiles as well as Jews to belong to his Church;
it was to be world-wide. So that, from the very
moment of its foundation, the Church *might* have been
called the Catholic Church. But as a matter of fact
it didn't, all at once, get that name. The name
" Catholic " didn't really come in till the fourth
century, the century of the great heresies, Arianism
and Nestorianism and what not. I don't want to
bother you at the moment about all those long names,
and still less about all the boring things they stood
for. But what I want to draw attention to is that
these heretics, these people who insisted on inventing
their own theology instead of letting the Church teach
them the doctrine she had received from the Apostles,
were always giving themselves away by being so
obviously provincial. They were provincial, whereas
the Church was Catholic.

What do I mean by " provincial "? Why, that they only represented one bit of the world. There were Nestorians, for example, in the east, in Asia Minor and so on, but there weren't any Nestorians in the west; but there were Catholics both in the east and in the west. There were Donatists in Africa, and there were Catholics in Africa; but there weren't any Donatists outside Africa, only Catholics. So that St. Augustine had a fairly easy job making the Donatists look foolish by asking them whether they really thought Jesus Christ only died for people living on the north coast of Africa. And, just about fifteen centuries later, a Church of England clergyman, reading about the history of the Donatist schism, got worried over that argument. If the Donatists could be made to look fools when you pointed out to them that they were very provincial sort of people, what about the Church of England? The very name " Church of England ", the very name " Anglican ", seemed to insist on the fact that this Church in which he had been born and bred was only a provincial Church, something different from the Catholic Church which Jesus Christ founded. So he gave up being a Church of England clergyman, and became John Henry Cardinal Newman instead. October the 9th is the anniversary of the day on which John Henry Newman knelt at the feet of an Italian Passionist who talked rather broken English, and abjured his heresy. So if you remember it by Saturday, which you won't, Saturday is a good day for you to say prayers for any Protestants you know whom you would like to see converted to the Catholic Faith.

The Catholic Church is everywhere, and the

Catholic Church is the same everywhere—that is her great mystery, that is the thing that bothers people outside the Church. They don't let you and me know it, but when you and I have gone out of the room they sit there wondering how on earth the Catholic Church holds together, and coming to the conclusion that there must be some catch about it. Because, if you come to think of it, it is very difficult to get two people to agree about *anything*. And the more members any Church or any society has, the more chance there is of disagreement. There is a story of an old lady in Scotland who thought all other Christians were wrong, and so started a Church of her own. And one day a caller, who was interested in her point of view, said, " Tell me, do you really believe, as people say you believe, that nobody will go to heaven except you and your coachman? " To which the old lady replied, " Weel, I'm no so sure about John ". It's easy to secure unanimity in a Church of that sort. But when you have a whole lot of members scattered all over the country, and still more when you have a whole lot of members scattered all over the world, the chances are enormous, humanly speaking, that they will start quarrelling about what is true doctrine and what is false doctrine. Or at least they will develop different ways of doing things; there will be two different theories about the way in which you ought to fold up a chasuble, and people will come to blows about that. So the spectacle of a Church which has members all over the world, all believing the same doctrines and all folding their chasubles more or less in the same way, makes the outside world very puzzled and suspicious. They shake their heads over us, and say,

" I expect, if we knew, these Catholics differ among themselves a good deal more than they let on ". Or else they will say, " These poor, wretched Catholics, ground down under the iron heel of Rome, never allowed for a moment to think for themselves! " There must be *some* catch about it.

Well, the immediate answer to that difficulty is a fairly obvious one. The reason why we Catholics don't quarrel about what we are to believe is that we accept the beliefs which have come down to us from the Apostles; we don't make up our theology as we go along. Catholic theology isn't made in Italy, or made in Germany, or made in France, or made in Spain, or made in Ireland; it was made in Palestine, nineteen centuries ago. But we shall have to consider all that more particularly a Sunday or two from now. It remains true that it *is* very remarkable the way the Catholic Church does manage to hold together, in spite of being a world-wide Church; because after all we Catholics are, by nature, as quarrelsome as most people. And I think these people who talk about our being ground down under the iron heel of Rome are making this mistake, principally—they don't realize the enormous personal loyalty which Catholics have for the Holy Father. It's rather like the way in which the British Empire holds together. The British Empire isn't ground down under the iron heel of Westminster; what really makes it hang together is that people in every part of the globe have a personal loyalty for King George the Sixth. And just in the same way people all over the globe have a personal loyalty for Pope Pius the Twelfth. Only in this case it is a supernatural loyalty. It is part of the grace you and I receive from our Communions, that we want, at all costs, to preserve the unity of the Church; and we see, in the person of the Holy Father, the symbol and the link which binds that unity together.

We were considering last Sunday why it is a good thing to belong to a Church. And I just want to point out now that it is a good thing to belong to a Catholic Church. It keeps you from getting too provincial in your outlook. We all of us have certain ways of looking at things because we are English—all except those of us who happen to be Irish or Polish or whatever it may be, and they have their own way of looking at things because they are Irish or Polish, so it comes to the same thing. But those of us who are English have our *own* national way of looking at things; we believe, for example, in free speech, and in taking exercise every afternoon, and in shooting pheasants but not shooting sparrows, and a whole lot of things like that. I haven't a word to say against all that; but I think it *is* useful to be a Catholic, to be a member of a Church which is as wide as mankind, and therefore to be able to remind yourself that not everybody thinks as you do; other people have their own national way of looking at things, just as you have yours. It helps you, I mean, not to be provincial-minded, if you belong to a Catholic Church.

Just in the same way, of course—though that is really rather outside our subject for this afternoon— it is a good thing to belong to a Church which can look back on nineteen centuries of existence; it helps you not to be too much impressed by the latest craze, the latest catchword. Just as many people around us are too English in their outlook, so many people around us are too twentieth-century in their outlook; it's only a different kind of provincialism really. The English Catholic has all the English instincts; and at the same time he or she, being a Catholic, is capable of getting *outside* that merely British point of view and seeing things as other people see them, as foreigners see them. An English Catholic going to Confession doesn't say, " I'm afraid I took no exercise on Wednesday or Thursday "; doesn't say, " I'm afraid I shot a sparrow yesterday "; doesn't fall into the mistake of imagining that the English way of looking at things is the only possible human way of looking at things.

So there you are, a Catholic. And, after all, being a Catholic has something to do with being broad-minded. I told you that the word Catholic means " all over the place ". When you say, " I am a Catholic ", you don't mean, " I am all over the place ". On the contrary, because you are a Catholic you know just where you stand. You know what you believe, and you know that yours is a world-wide belief. You don't have to pull yourself up and wonder whether it's just because you are English that you think it's wrong to lie, or to steal, if it's just a matter of national habit, like taking exercise in the afternoon. No, you are a Catholic, and if you were an Eskimo or a Hottentot you would still be a Catholic, and you would still think it wrong to lie or steal. So you know where you are. But just because you know where you are, you ought to try and see, to try and understand, the point of view of people who differ from you. And especially, because you belong to a world-wide Church, you ought to try and understand the point of view of *nations* other than your own. You oughtn't to dig yourself in behind a lot of English prejudices and contemptuously dismiss the whole of the rest of the world as " foreigners ". I always remember during the last war, when the idea of having a League of Nations first came up, one of our newspapers assuring its readers that the British nation would never have anything to do with a League of Nations in which foreigners were in the majority. That is the sort of spirit you have got to try and get out of, if you are going to be good and useful citizens in the very odd and confused world into which you are growing up. You believe in the Catholic Church, and your sympathies, your outlook, should be not less world-wide than hers.

XXII

I believe in the holy Catholic Church (4)

WE REALLY must get on with this particular article in the *Credo*, so I'm going to force the pace a bit today and see if we can't finish.

In the *Credo* which is said at Mass—I don't know if any of you follow it in your books—the Church is described in four ways; she is one and apostolic, as well as holy and Catholic. We've talked about the unity of the Church; now, what do we mean by calling her apostolic? It's an ugly word, vaguely suggesting carbolic soap; but its meaning is quite simple, it means that she has come down to us straight, and unaltered, from the Apostles. Why did they leave that out in the Apostles' Creed? Well, of course, the old story used to be that the Apostles themselves made up the Apostles' Creed, each of them doing one clause like a sort of round game. If that really happened, you could understand why they didn't say the Church had come down to them from the Apostles, because they *were* the Apostles. But I fancy clever people nowadays say that story isn't true. All the same, the Apostles' Creed comes down to us from very early times; and if you want proof of that, you have only to consider the fact that they didn't bother to mention the Church was one, or that it was apostolic. Because in the very early Church there had been no big quarrels or divisions between Christians, so it seemed silly to say the Church was one; it was like saying, " Pigs can't fly ". And there wasn't much point in saying it came down from the Apostles, when the Apostles had only just died the other day. That is the sort of consideration clever people never seem to think of.

Anyhow, the Church is apostolic, and we don't understand fully what the Church means until we take that into account. So let's get it clear. The faith which we hold was the faith held by the Apostles. You see, the chief reason why our Lord wanted to have Apostles at all was so that they could be his *witnesses* after he had gone back into heaven; they would be able to remember what he had said, and to tell other people. Everything we know about our Lord comes down from those Apostles of his—nobody else was going to tell us about it. The Jews weren't going to leave us an account of how they had crucified him. The Romans weren't going to bother about somebody whom they regarded as an unimportant religious fanatic in a very one-horse province like Judaea. So our Lord's own friends had to tell us about it, or nobody would. And we are not to imagine that all our Lord said to his Apostles is written down in the Bible. If you read out loud all the remarks our Lord makes to his Apostles in the Gospels, for example, how long do you suppose it would take? Perhaps a couple of hours. And our Lord was living with his Apostles for three years before his crucifixion, and after he had risen from the dead he came to them, not once, but several times, and talked to them, we are told, about the things pertaining to the kingdom of God.

And I do hope some of you are remembering by now that when he refers to the kingdom of God he means his Church. So there were lots and lots of things he must have said which have never come down to us in writing at all. He told his Apostles all that we Christians need to know, and they passed it on to their own disciples, and they to *their* disciples, and so the thing has gone on till it has reached you and me.

Of course when I say that I don't mean that our Lord used exactly the theological language we use nowadays when he taught his disciples. They were only peasant people from Galilee, and you can see from the sort of things they say in the Gospels that they were apt to be pretty stupid at that. I don't know whether you think that I use very long words and very unintelligible expressions when I preach to you on Sunday afternoons like this? Believe me, it might be very much worse. Let's try, and see how you like it. What was I saying? Oh, yes—" When we predicate a substantial identity between the un-recorded but validly hypothecated indoctrination of those Palestinian seminarians with the easily assimilable rudiments of primitive symbolism, and the highly organized and differentiated system of soteriology which adapts itself to the conceptual receptivity of a more intellectualized epoch, we must be understood as referring rather to a progressive accuracy of formulation than to any expansion or even (what is equivocally designated) explication of the content actually (though in a sense germinally) present to the former entity." All that sentence is perfectly sound theology, and it's all English, though perhaps not very basic English, but anybody who understood it is welcome to hold up her hand. There you are, you see; I don't preach to you like that, and our Lord didn't preach like that to his Apostles. He gave them just the big idea, the marrow of Christian theology, explained in simple terms, and left it for later Christians to work it out more elaborately when need arose. If you'd asked St. Peter, for example, what was meant by the Hypostatic Union, he would probably have said, " You can search me ".

I say, later Christians were to work it out more elaborately when need arose; why should it arise? Why, because of heresy; because if you aren't careful ingenious people will always invent wrong explanations, which have the effect of explaining things away. And that's what kept on happening with Christian theology. One heretic would explain the doctrine of the Trinity by saying that there were three Gods, and then another would explain it by saying that there was one God whom you could call by three different names. And in order to make it clear to both of them that they were wrong, you had to talk to them about three Persons and one Substance. I don't imagine our Lord talked to his Apostles about Persons and Substance; he didn't have to. But as time goes on and people will try to explain things, you have to state your meaning more and more accurately, more and more precisely; that's why the Nicene Creed which we say at Mass is longer than the Apostles' Creed, which was composed much earlier—there were more heresies to be guarded against. It's rather like sharpening a pencil. If you just want to write " Mary Jane is an ass " in somebody's exercise book, any sort of point will do, but if you're going to draw nice circles in geometry you've got to sharpen it. So the definitions of the Christian faith had to be sharpened as time went on. Only the creed didn't get smaller and smaller, like the point of a pencil. It got larger and larger, like a balloon which you blow up and blow up, but it's the same balloon all the time.

But now, how are we to be certain that the Church hasn't cheated; that *she* hasn't given us wrong explanations of Christian doctrine? For instance, there was a heretic called Nestorius who said that the eternal Son of God and Jesus of Nazareth were two different Persons. Well, we know that that's wrong; we know that our Lord had two different natures, but the nature of the Son of God and the nature of Jesus of Nazareth belong to the same Person. Yes, but how do we know that the Church was right and Nestorius was wrong? That's the next point; we know that because we believe that the Church is infallible. When she makes up her mind on a point of doctrine like that, God doesn't let her make a mistake; that's what infallibility means. It doesn't mean that when Mother Dominic is teaching you history she can't possibly get a date wrong. It doesn't mean that Ireland was necessarily right to keep out of the war, or that Portugal was necessarily right to come into the war. Any single Catholic may be wrong, and any casual collection of Catholics may be wrong. But when the bishops of the Catholic Church meet in a council, and sit down to decide what the true notion of the Catholic Church is, they can't possibly go wrong. God won't let them; that's infallibility.

Obviously that idea of holding a general council is the best way to find out the truth about any Christian doctrine. Because the bishops come from all over the world, and each can testify to what the Christian tradition is in his part of the world, and as far as he knows always has been. In the early councils, for instance, the bishop of Alexandria would get up and say, " This is what my predecessor St. Mark used to teach ", and the Bishop of Ephesus could get up and say, " This is what my predecessor St. John used to teach ", and so on. But there's one difficulty about it. Bishops are mostly elderly people, and travelling isn't good for them, and they don't like leaving their dioceses with nobody to look after them, and therefore it isn't possible to hold a general council very often. I think I'm right in saying that there was no general council between the council of Trent, which happened in the time of Queen Elizabeth, when Raleigh had just learned to smoke and Shakespeare was a promising young dramatist, and the Vatican Council, which happened in the time of Queen Victoria, when your grandfathers were still pretty young. Three hundred years is a long gap; and was it impossible, during all those three hundred years, to find out what the truth about any disputed Christian doctrine was? No, it wasn't impossible. Because our Lord has arranged that the bishop of one particular diocese in the world should be infallible, just as the Church is infallible. And that is the successor of St. Peter, the bishop of Rome.

Not, of course, that it is impossible for the pope to be wrong about casual points of fact, about where he left his spectacles, for example, just as much as you or me. Even in official sort of documents, the pope isn't always right; I was reading the other day about a bull

published by Pope Gregory the Ninth, which began,
" Now that the evening of the world is drawing to a
close "; and that was seven hundred years ago, and
the world hasn't come to an end yet. No, but when the
pope decides to make up his mind about something,
as the supreme Teacher of all Christians, and takes
the best advice he can and goes into all that is known
about Christian tradition on the subject, and solemnly
invokes the Holy Spirit, and then gets on to his
throne and gives out what he is going to give out as
Divine truth, then the pope is infallible.

So one job which the pope has is to teach you and
me, when occasion arises. Another job which he has
got, as the successor of the Apostles, is to govern you
and me. The Church is our Mother, and, being our
Mother, she not only tells us what's what, she tells
us what to do. If she tells us not to eat meat on
Fridays, we've not got to eat meat on Fridays, and
that's that. And the pope is the Head of the Universal
Church; so if he tells us to say the rosary at Benediction all through October, we've got to say the
rosary at Benediction all through October, and, once
more, that's that. Mark you, I don't say that in the
first centuries the popes laid down laws for the
universal Church as freely as they do now; they
hadn't got the opportunity. Christians were very
scattered, and the pope himself was a persecuted out-
law living in the cellars underneath Rome; and he
hadn't got a telephone or a wireless station as he has
now. The *unity* of the Church has never ceased, from
the day of Pentecost to this. The *uniformity* of the
Church is a thing which has, to some extent, grown
up. Not that the pope hadn't always the power to

interfere if he wanted to. If he was the Rock on which the faith of the Church was built, he also had the keys of the kingdom of heaven entrusted to him, and if he excommunicated anybody, it went. But in those first days he had quite enough to do looking after Italy, and in other parts of the world the local bishops ran things more or less in their own way, until the Church grew, and her vast unity became a thing too complicated for that.

And there is one other point I would like to mention, because it is always cropping up when you are talking to Protestants. People say, " Couldn't the pope see Hitler was wrong? And if he could, why didn't he tell all the Catholics in Germany to stop fighting and make Hitler look a fool? " Well, don't let's allow them to get away with it too easily. We are not *bound* to say that the Holy Father has been right in keeping silence, on the whole, about which side was in the right and which side was in the wrong. It *may* have been an error of judgement, and there is no Divine promise of infallibility to protect him against that. " But as a matter of fact," we shall be inclined to add, " I don't think he was wrong." You see, popes don't like to interfere too much in politics, especially international politics, if they can help it. Partly because it is not so easy to be certain which side is in the right, when you are hearing the propaganda from the wrong side all the time—and remember, the Holy Father had been doing that all through the war. Partly because it would have been putting too big a strain on the consciences of the German Catholics. The pious ones would have refused to fight, and got shot; the unpious ones would have fought, and incurred the guilt of disobeying their spiritual ruler; and the betwixts and betweens wouldn't have known what to do, and would have fought one day and thrown down their arms the next, and altogether it would have been very confusing. The one certain thing is, it wouldn't have stopped Hitler.

I'm afraid I've tried to crowd in an awful lot today, but I felt we must be getting on, for the sake of people who are leaving in the summer, so next Sunday we'll start fair on the Communion of Saints.

XXIII

The Communion of Saints (1)

IT'S A VERY odd thing, but if you had asked St. Paul
what he meant by " the Communion of Saints ",
I think he would have said, without much hesitation,
" I mean that when one set of Christians is hard up
another set of Christians, in a different part of the
world, sends round the hat and takes up a collection
for them ".

That principle of give and take between Christians
is a very good illustration of what *we* mean by the
Communion of Saints. The Church is divided into
three large bits; part of it is on earth, part of it is in
heaven, part of it is in Purgatory. The Church in
heaven is All Saints. The Church in Purgatory is
All Souls. The Church on earth is all sorts. We, on
earth, are poorer than the saints in heaven, so we ask
them to give us something. But we, on earth, are
richer than the souls in Purgatory, so they ask us to
give them something. It's the same old principle St.
Paul used to preach, of give and take between
Christians all round.

Some people, when they die, go straight to heaven.
Suppose an atheist gets baptized, and then gets killed
in an air-raid on his way home, he has to go straight
to heaven; there's nothing to prevent it. His sins have
all been forgiven, and there he is. You may think

it's rather bad luck on you that you were baptized when you were quite small, so you haven't got the same chances. Still, if you were to get a plenary indulgence just before you died—which involves not only being sorry for your sins, but being without any affection for your sins, which isn't so easy—you would go straight to heaven. And I expect one way and another there are a lot of people there. Some, no doubt, have been through their Purgatory and got finished with it, and now they're in heaven just the same. I should think there are lots and lots of people in heaven. And last Monday's feast—I hope the nuns remembered to make you all go to Mass, because it's a very important feast—was All Saints' Day, which is meant to remind us of that. In some ways I think it's the jolliest feast in the year. Crowds and crowds and crowds of people all perfectly happy, and all doing God's will without having to think twice about it.

Among those people are some who didn't just scrape in by happening to die at exactly the right moment; who didn't have to wade through Purgatory to get there. They are God's special friends, people who spent a whole life-time, many of them, trying to please him, and who died, many of them, most uncomfortable deaths for love of him. We don't know all their names by any means. The Church says she can tell us the names of some of them, and she canonizes them. That is to say, some time after they are dead she holds a kind of inquest on them; and somebody gets up and says what wonderful people they were and somebody else gets up—he has to do it, because he's paid to—and tries to pick holes in their characters. That doesn't sound a very nice thing to do, because it's beastly to pick holes in people's characters even when they are alive. But it's this man's job to do it, and it's all right because he's only trying to make sure that the other man can prove his case. And if she's satisfied at the result of that process, the Church tells us we can be *certain* that this particular soul has gone to heaven, and we put " St." in front of the person's name and all the rest of it. Mark this, I think there are probably lots of saints whom the Church never does canonize. Lots of people, I mean, who are real friends of God and live very very holy lives without anybody taking much notice; and when they die they go straight to heaven and shine there with a glory not less than some of those others—only God didn't wish them, for some reason, to be known as saints on earth.

The floor of heaven is like a window with a muslin curtain across it; we can't see in, but the saints can see out. They see what we are doing, and are interested in what we are doing; the Epistle to the Hebrews compares them to spectators looking on at a race. If you are ever feeling rather down-hearted about your second-rate efforts to live a good Christian life, think of the saints in heaven bending over the balconies in front of them and shouting out " Stick it! " as people do when they are watching a race. As I say, there are lots of people in heaven who are not canonized Saints, and there is nothing to prevent you, if you want to, asking for the prayers of any good person you've known or read about; they may be in heaven already. But, if you want to be on the safe side, you ask for the prayers of somebody who is CERTAINLY in heaven—the Church has told us so. The

Saints are the rich people, you see, helping out the needs of us, their brothers and sisters, who are poor. They are rich in *merits*; that is, they have a high claim to a reward from God for all the holy things they did and all the uncomfortable things they suffered for love of him. I dare say some of you have rich uncles who give you tips in the holidays; and this is the same sort of idea, only the way the Saints do it is to pray to God for us, and get him to give us the graces we need.

And the richest of all, and surely the most generous of all, is our blessed Lady. It's odd how we all think of her as a special friend, isn't it? I mean, if you were called Emerentiana, or Eustochium (which sounds like a boy's name, but it's a girl's name really), you could say " Dear St. Emerentiana, or Dear St. Eustochium, do please pray for me " when you were in a tight place, and feel fairly certain that your patron saint, whichever it was, would be listening, because there couldn't be very many people of that name praying to her at that particular moment. It seems much more odd that we should pray with such confidence to our blessed Lady, who must be deafened, one would think, with the sound of " Hail, Mary's " going up all over the world. But we're quite right. You, as a Christian, are the sister of Jesus Christ, and therefore our Lady is your Mother. I suppose it was because he wanted us to see that that our Lord gave her to St. John from the Cross. He didn't talk much on the Cross; he was in terrible pain, you see, and every word cost him an effort; after " Father forgive them, for they know not what they do " he only said twenty-two words altogether. But five of those words were

addressed to our Lady, and to St. John, the baby of the
Apostles, who stood there with her; " Behold thy
Mother " was meant for every Christian. So we all
treat her as if she belonged to us; one always does
treat one's mother like that.

Those are our rich friends, then, the people in
heaven. And if they are so generous to us with their
prayers, you and I ought to be generous with our
prayers for our poor friends, the poor souls in Purgatory. We always do think of them, don't we, as the
poor souls in Purgatory. That seems curious, from
one point of view; from one point of view they are
so much better off than we are. You and I might go
to hell; they can't. We sometimes think of them
enviously, for that reason. They are like friends who
have gone on ahead, and successfully jumped over the
precipice that lay in our path; we haven't jumped it yet
—how much better off they are than we! Yes, but
from another point of view they are hard up, the holy
souls, desperately hard up. We can still merit; they
can't. Nothing they can do can give them any relief,
can bring them any nearer to the heaven which is their
only desire, their only dream. If you will, they are
like people who have got plenty of money at the bank,
but no cash in their pockets; what is the use of money
if one can't get at it? So they ask for our prayers,
which can help them; our prayers, which we ought to
give generously, just as the Saints give their prayers
to us. So, each year, November reminds us about the
Communion of Saints; about the help we can get,
about the help we can give. You remember the
fable about the lion which was caught in a net, and the
mouse that helped it by eating through the net so that

it could get out? You and I are like that when we pray for the souls of Christians departed. They are much more splendid people than you and I are; they are already on the last lap of their journey home. But they are held up on that journey, and they can't help themselves; we can help them, and it isn't presumptuous to think of ourselves as helping them, even splendid people who have fallen gloriously in battle—we are the mice nibbling away at the bonds which hold them, that is all.

XXIV

The Communion of Saints (2)

I DARE say that last Sunday, when I was talking about this subject, one or two of you were asking yourselves, " Why on earth isn't he saying anything about Holy Communion? " And I must admit that, unlike many of the questions which suggest themselves to your minds, that is a fairly reasonable one. It isn't, surely, a mere accident that we use the same word, communion, to describe the bond which unites us all as Christians, and to describe the Sacrament of our Lord's Body and Blood. For the time being let's leave out of sight one side of the matter with which we were particularly occupied last Sunday, because it happened to be the first Sunday in November; I mean the fellowship which we Christian people enjoy, through faith, with our dead; with the souls waiting in Purgatory and the souls already crowned in heaven. Let's think only of the Church on earth, and ask ourselves what is the bond which really ties Christian people together, here on earth.

Our Lord Jesus Christ was very anxious that Christians should love one another. He knew that that didn't come natural to us, since our nature was spoilt by the Fall. He knew that one's natural instinct was not to love the girl at the next desk or the girl in the next bed, but to tease her and wish we got as many marks as she did and criticize the way she does her hair. So he thought, " I won't just *tell* them to love one another; I'm tired of telling them to do things which they don't do all the same. I'm going to *help* them to love one another, and the best way to do that will be to give them grace to do it through one of my Sacraments ". And the Sacrament he chose for that purpose was the Sacrament of Holy Eucharist. The grace of the Holy Eucharist helps us to love God; but we seem to forget that it *also* helps us, if we use it properly, to love one another.

And that's quite reasonable. Because, after all, sharing the same food is a natural symbol of friendship. Not if you're thinking of animals; if you give two guinea-pigs one piece of lettuce or whatever it is guinea-pigs eat, the bigger one gets most of it and there's no love lost over that. And I dare say human beings sometimes feel badly about it if they think the girl next them has been given a bigger helping. No, but the old kind of family meal did bring with it the sense of a family reunion. Papa was carving and Mamma got half the breast and the eldest got the other half and then the next two got the wings and you were left with one of the legs, which was rather annoying, but it was all right because it was all the same chicken. Day after day you shared the same food, and it drove home to you the fact that you were a single family. Nowadays, when you go into a snack bar and scoop up a bit of spam and a couple of parsnips for yourself, I dare say it's different. But I'm talking of old days. And I suppose there is no doubt that the model which our Lord had in mind was the feast of the Pasch, as the Jews kept it. One lamb for the whole household; plenty to go round, even in those days of big families. It was, I suppose, to them something like what the Christmas dinner is to us; it was a festival of home reunion. And our Lord said, " My friends shall have a feast of home reunion like that. Only it shan't happen just one day in the year, it shall happen all the year round. And it shan't be a common meal for one family here, and a common meal for another family there. *All* my friends shall be one family, and have one common meal, going on *all* over the world, going on *all* the year round ". So he instituted the Holy Eucharist.

And it wasn't to be just like the other sacraments; they are marvellous enough, but this was to be something more marvellous still. It's very extraordinary that a few drops of water which would hardly be enough to wash your face with at night should wash away all your sins; but it does, in baptism. It's very extraordinary that one or two smudges of oil which wouldn't be enough to make a midge-bite stop itching should prepare a man against the approach of death; but they do, in extreme unction. It's very extraordinary how these material things can convey Divine grace, but the things *themselves* remain unaltered. If you get a cheque signed by your papa which says, " Pay Mary Jane five pounds ", and take it to a bank, you can get five pounds for it, but the piece of paper is only a piece of paper still. So in baptism the water is only plain water; in extreme unction the oil is only plain oil. But in the sacrament of Holy Eucharist, as we know, the Bread and Wine aren't just plain bread and wine; indeed, they aren't strictly speaking bread and wine at all. Something has happened to them, they've turned into something different. That's why I say this sacrament is so much more remarkable than all the other sacraments.

Let's just remind ourselves about that again. I was talking about it last summer, but some of you weren't here. The simplest way to put it is that our Lord's presence in the Holy Eucharist is just the opposite of your presence in the looking-glass. When you brush your hair in front of the looking-glass, those of you who haven't thrown your brushes out into the lavender, the girl opposite, in the looking-glass, has the same *appearance* as you, but she has no reality; it *looks* like you, but it *isn't* you. When you were looking, just now, at the sacred Host in the monstrance, it hadn't the *appearance* of Jesus Christ, but it had the reality; it didn't *look* like him, but it *was* him. The substance that lies behind the appearances of bread and wine is there no longer after the Consecration; Jesus Christ himself is present there instead. And he comes right into us, unites us bodily with himself; why does he do that?

Well, of course there are all sorts of reasons. He does it so as to increase the love of God in our souls. He does it so as to make us less interested in worldly pleasures and worldly anxieties, so as to tune our hearts to the music of heaven. He does it so as to make us strong against the assaults of temptation, just as bodily food makes us strong to resist the assaults of disease. But there is one particular reason I want to draw your attention to this afternoon, partly because we so often forget about it, and partly because it's what I set out to talk about. He comes to you and me, to each of us, so that we may feel he has come to *all* of us. And feeling that, you and I ought to feel drawn closer together, all of us. We are all united to him, and therefore we are all united to one another.

You see what I mean—even if this sacrament had been just like the other sacraments, it would have been quite obvious, I think, that it was meant to be a bond of union between us all. Suppose, for the moment, that there was no such thing as Transubstantiation. Suppose that you and I, when we went to Communion, received a small round piece of unleavened bread, that and nothing more. Even so, it would be a sacrament; that round piece of unleavened bread would confer grace on us, every bit as much as water does in baptism, or oil in extreme unction. And we should say to ourselves, " Here was I, this morning, receiving a piece of bread, exactly like the person next me and receiving exactly the same grace from it as she did; it wouldn't do to call her a nasty stuck-up toad after that ". But, you see, it isn't like that. It isn't simply that you've received something exactly *like* what she received; you've received exactly the *same* thing which she received, the Body and Blood of our Lord Jesus Christ. It isn't as if you had received one part of Christ and she another. Each of you received the whole of Christ, each became part of him, in making him part of herself—that is what Transubstantiation means. Each of you has been united, sacramentally, with one Person; all of you, then, have *become one Person* in Jesus Christ.

And there's another thing which makes the sacrament of Holy Eucharist different from all the other sacraments; it is an action, whereas they are only transactions. What on earth do I mean by that?

Why, by an action I mean something that you do for the sake of doing it; by a transaction I mean something you do for the sake of getting it done. When you go out skating, for example, you do it for the sake of doing it; you spin it out as much as possible; you don't say " Thank goodness that's over " when you've finished—that is an *action*. But a transaction is like, say, having your hair cut. Perhaps I'm wrong about that; perhaps you do enjoy having your hair done, and all that nice oozy feeling of being shampooed. But I'm talking of myself now; and when *I* get my hair cut I like to get it over as soon as possible. I go into the shop with my hair long, and I want to come out again with my hair short; and the less time the barber wastes in between, by chatting and going to look out of the window and snipping vaguely round the edges, the better I'm pleased. That's a transaction.

Now, most of the sacraments, if we may say it without irreverence, are transactions; you are doing something for the sake of getting it done. When you go to confession, for example, you go in feeling guilty and you want to come out again feeling innocent, and the sooner that happens the better you're pleased. Of course, there again I may be wrong; some of you may be going to grow up into the sort of ladies who enjoy going round to the nearest big church and spending half an hour talking to the priest about their souls. But most of us, I think, have rather different ideas about it; we like to be in the position of the Irishman who knew the parish priest very well, and the parish priest knew *him* very well, so whenever he went into the box the priest used to say, " Well, Pat,

same old sins? " and he said, " Yes, your Reverence ",
and the priest used to say, " Very well, Pat, same old
penance ", and that was that. It's the same with the
other sacraments; baptism does take a good long time,
but everybody there, really, is wanting to get it over
as soon as possible, including the baby. And Confirmation is the same; you may, of course, get a
longish sermon from the bishop, but that, you feel, is
just bad luck; the ceremony itself takes about ten
minutes, and that's about what we want it to take.
And if you ever get married I expect you'll find the
same about the wedding. The Church's instinct
about sacraments is always, " It's got to be done, so
let's get it over as soon as possible ".

But not about the Holy Eucharist. Because the
Holy Eucharist is really a part of the Mass, and the
Mass isn't just a transaction; it's an action. It's
true you can go to Communion outside of Mass,
when that's the only manageable way of doing it ;
but going to Communion is really part of Mass, and
the Mass is an action. The Mass, you see, is not
only a sacrament, but a sacrifice. It is a supreme act
of worship which we are privileged to offer to God,
and we don't want it to be all over in ten minutes; we
want to spin it out and make the most of it. Our Lord
hung on the Cross for three hours offering himself
as a sacrifice for us, and wherever and whenever Mass
is celebrated he renews that action of his. When a
composer makes up a tune, in a sense that's all over
and done; there's the tune, finished. But people can
go on playing that tune day after day, renewing it by
performing it afresh. So with our Lord's sacrifice
on Calvary; in a sense it was all over and done; there

was the sacrifice, finished. But priests can go on saying Mass, day after day, renewing that sacrifice by performing it afresh. And whenever that happens, we naturally want to be there, joining with the priest in this splendid act of worship. It's something we want to *do*, not something we want to get done.

And, once again, that brings us back to the Communion of Saints. Because this sacrifice, this action of ours, is a common action, we are all doing it together. You may have noticed that I turn round and say something inaudible just at the moment when you are putting your penny into the plate, or dropping it on the floor as the case may be. What I am saying is this, " Pray, brethren, that my sacrifice AND YOURS may be acceptable before Almighty God ". My sacrifice and yours—it's true that if I go to bed suddenly with a cold you don't get Mass in the morning. You can't have Mass without a priest, any more than you can have skating without ice. But it's *your* sacrifice as much as mine; and it's a common effort. You are doing your part of that effort, as long as you are saying your prayers and not looking round and giggling. You don't need to say, " I'm going to ring the sanctus-bell "; the sanctus-bell isn't what God is waiting to hear, it's the prayers of each of you, the prayers of all of you. In one great sigh of prayer you are—you ought to be—united every time you go to Mass.

And the Mass is not merely the common sacrifice of this particular rather jolly lot of people living at Aldenham. It's the sacrifice of the whole Church; in the very middle of it we pray for the pope, and for all good Christians who observe the Catholic and

Apostolic faith. We pray, a bit later, for all the dead who are at rest in Christ. We join ourselves in Communion with our Blessed Lady and all the Apostles and a whole string of Saints besides; we pray that we may have part and lot with St. Felicity, and St. Perpetua, and St. Agatha, and St. Lucy, and St. Agnes (aged thirteen), and St. Cecily, and St. Anastasia, and all the Saints. So, once again, we find ourselves at one with the living and the dead; there is a rush and a stir about us of the angels' wings, and we hear the hum and bustle of the Church's prayer, all part of ours, and ours part of it. And then we go to Communion.

XXV

The forgiveness of sins (1)

I HOPE you won't think that, in preaching these sermons to you, I'm trying to make things more difficult for you, and suggest a lot of difficulties about religion which would never have occurred to you if I hadn't mentioned them. In a way, of course, I am doing that; but my reason for doing it is that if I didn't suggest these difficulties now they would probably suggest themselves to you later, and then you might have nobody to go and talk to about them and find out what the answers were. The forgiveness of sins, for example, how nice and easy that sounds when we've been accustomed all our lives to ask God for forgiveness, and get it in the confessional! But it isn't really so nice and easy as all that; it's a very difficult notion to understand, when you come to look into it.

It seems easy to us because our Lord taught us to say, " Forgive us our trespasses, as we forgive them that trespass against us ". We are all quite accustomed to forgiving people, at least I hope we are; so why shouldn't God find it just as easy as we do? Let's suppose, for example, that somebody has been beastly to you. Let's suppose that she's got into a temper and said all sorts of unkind things to you— I mean one of your friends, of course; I don't mean the mistresses; that's what they are there for. And then her temper got ungovernable and she did something really dreadful, pulled your hair or something like that. Well, after a bit she comes back rather miserable, and tells you she's sorry. I expect you'd probably forgive her. There would be all sorts of reasons for forgiving her. One is, you're rather a slack person by nature and you don't want all the bother of keeping up a feud for the rest of the term. Another is that you rather want to move in the best circles, and she moves in rather better circles than you, so it would be a pity to have her against you; you are even a bit frightened of her, perhaps, because she's bigger than you. Or again, you reflect that after all there's no great harm done, and you'd have had to do your hair before tea, anyhow. Or possibly even you reflect (this would be much nicer of you, and much more supernatural of you) that you aren't a person of enormous importance in the world, and it would be silly to take up an attitude of injured dignity when you haven't, when all's said and done, very much dignity to injure. One way and another, you forgive her.

And then you say, " Well, if I can behave like that, why can't God? " Yes, but remember, he has none of your reasons, the reasons we mentioned just now. God isn't a sort of easy-going person who finds it more comfortable to forget about grievances—he can't forget. God doesn't expect any advantage, or get any advantage, from keeping on the right side of his creatures, of people like you and me. And there *is* great harm done when we offend God by any grave sin; the whole order of nature has been turned upside down when the creature revolts like that against its Creator. And God's dignity is infinite, so there can be no question of his forgiving us because his dignity doesn't very much matter. So we were wrong if we thought it was all quite plain sailing like that. We mustn't get into the habit of thinking that God is a good-humoured sort of Person whom it's quite easy to talk round if you use a bit of soft soap, so that you can spend your life doing things he has told you not to and then going and making it up with him every Saturday night.

Well, now look at it from another point of view; think what it must be like to be a judge, and have to punish people for serious crimes—not because they have annoyed *you*, but because they have offended against the law of the land. Or take an extreme case; suppose at the end of the war, when Germany was beaten and all that, the Prime Minister and President Roosevelt and Mr. Stalin got together to decide what they were going to do with Hitler. And suppose they argued and argued and argued about it and couldn't agree what to do till at last the Prime Minister said, " Well, there's obviously only one way out of it; we must leave it to Mary Jane ". Now, what are you going to do about it? You can't take the line that after all Hitler hasn't done much harm to you and you rather like his moustache, and perhaps it would about meet the case if he lost his recompense. Because you are *judging*, and you are judging a man who, quite probably, has been responsible for more misery than any man who ever went before him. Mind you, I'm not telling you what you ought to do; you might think he ought to be shot, or you might say he'd got to spend the rest of his life on Pantelleria or one of those islands. But you'd feel, I think, that you couldn't just *forgive him*; a great wrong has been done, and something has got to happen in order to redress the balance of justice. And if Hitler were brought up the drive in one of those carts they take the cattle about in, and appealed to you personally to let him out, swearing he was sorry for what he had done and that he wouldn't do it again, you still couldn't just forgive him. Justice, *somehow*, has got to be done.

Now reflect that God is there to judge us for all the sins we commit against the eternal order of justice, and ask yourself, " How is it that he ever forgives? How can he consent to treat us as innocent, when he knows we have been guilty of these things? How can he condone the wrong, just because we say we are sorry and will try not to do it again? The wrong has been done, all the same; our tears can't wash out the record of it ". How did he ever forgive St. Paul who, when he was a young man, had gone about putting Christians to death? St. Paul might say he was sorry, but that wouldn't bring the Christians to life again. When we think of God as a Person whom our sins have annoyed, it's quite natural to imagine him being indulgent with us. Like the story of the girl who told her mother she had met a lion on her afternoon walk, and her mother said it was wicked to tell lies like that, and she must go and ask God to forgive her. So when the girl came down to tea, the Mamma said, " Did you tell God you were sorry? " and she said, " Yes, I did, and he said, ' Don't mention it, Miss Jones, I'm always mistaking that yellow dog for

a lion myself ' ". If we get into the habit of thinking
of our sins like that, as I say, it makes us careless
about them. But if we go to the other extreme, and
think of our sins as having fatally disturbed the
balance of Divine justice, we find ourselves wondering
whether it's possible even for God himself to forgive
sins, and that makes us get scrupulous and perhaps
fall into despair.

So we've got to accept the forgiveness of sins as
one of the great mysteries of our religion. Our sins
are real, and they are horrible; and yet God, who is
infinite Justice, can forgive them. He does forgive
them, if only we will repent, by which I mean not just
say that we're sorry, but take the trouble to make ourselves feel sorry—we shall have to talk a bit about
that later on. And the reason why he forgives us is
because, as we were saying about a couple of terms
ago, our Lord Jesus Christ made satisfaction for our
sins on the Cross, hanging there as the Head and
the Representative of humanity, making amends for
our sins. That's all we can know, I think, about the
process by which God forgives us; it will remain a
mystery to the end of time.

And now, about the effects of God's forgiveness;
that's rather a mystery, too. Go back for a moment to
what we were talking about at the beginning of this
sermon, think what happens when another person
has been beastly to you, and you forgive her. The
effect of that forgiveness is to make a change in
you, not in her; *you* have become a nicer person than
you were. You *were* in a bad temper, now you are in
a good temper; you were stuffy when you met her,
now you can afford to be unstuffy; you used to turn

up your nose at her, now you can turn it down again. But when God forgives us, it's the other way about. It isn't that God becomes a nicer Person; he couldn't be nicer than he is. But *we*, the people he forgives, become nicer people; it makes a change in *us*. Let's get that clear for a moment.

Some things that we do leave a mark behind them, and some don't. For instance, if you're standing by the Shore Pool, and throw a stone at one of the ducks —which isn't a very nice thing to do, but some of you might do it in your less ladylike moments—the duck doesn't mind, because of course it hasn't gone anywhere near the duck, the stone sinks, and there are some rather jolly ripples which mark, for a few moments, the place where it sank. After that, the surface of the pool is exactly like what it was before; there are you looking as good as gold, and nobody could possibly tell what you had been up to. But if, now—let's think of something really dreadful. Supposing you are walking along the passage with an enormous pile of books in your arms, more or less wedged in at the top by your chin; and supposing that on the top of the books you are carrying an ink-pot. And then, as usual, you try to take the corners at sixty miles an hour, and you run into somebody, and the whole lot comes down. And the ink-pot, very cleverly made so as to be unspillable, isn't quite prepared for that sort of test, so there's a horrid great stream of black left on the floor. Well, you do your best with blotting-paper, but it doesn't really amount to very much; the next nun who passes will have no difficulty in seeing what has been happening there, however good you look. This time, what you did has left a black mark. I don't mean merely that it has left a black mark against your record and you will probably have to write in pencil for the rest of the term. I mean there's a great beastly black mark on the floor, and Sister Oswin will have to come along with a bucket and wash the stain out before the passage looks respectable again.

Now, when you and I commit sin, it isn't like throwing that stone into the Shore Pool, it's like dropping that ink-pot; it leaves a mark. I don't merely mean that God writes up a bad mark, so to speak, against our record; sin leaves its mark on our souls. Of course, when we say that, it's only what clever people call an analogy; our souls are not material, like our bodies, and you can't get your soul stained with ink as you get your hands stained with ink. But something happens to your soul when you sin; it becomes different from what it was before, like the oil-cloth in the passage, not like the surface of the shore pool. And here is the thing we've got to remember; when God forgives us our sins, that mark comes out. When you forgive somebody who has offended you, a change takes place in you, the forgiver. But when you have offended God and he forgives you, the change takes place not in him, the Forgiver, but in you, the forgiven. The mark has come out, and your soul is as beautiful as if you had never sinned at all. Luther would have it that when God forgives us he doesn't take away our sins, he only hides them away, takes no notice of them and pretends that they aren't there. Which is just as if Sister Oswin were to put down a square of carpet on the place where you spilt the ink, instead of getting to work with that bucket.

That's heresy; when we say " I believe in the forgiveness of sins ", we mean that sins are really taken away by absolution; that everything is just as it was before.

When I say everything, it's well to remark that there are certain effects of sin which live on, even when the sins themselves have been forgiven. For one thing, every bad action of ours helps to get us into bad habits. It's like biting your nails, if you will pardon me for mentioning such an unladylike subject. Every time the nail-biter bites his nails, the more chances there are that he will do it next time he isn't thinking; he is getting into a habit of it. And so it is with our sinful habits; every time the drunkard gets drunk, the more chances there are that he will get drunk next time he finds himself with a mug in his hand; he is getting into the habit of it. So it is, even with the sins where our bodies are not concerned; every time you say something spiteful about a person you don't like you are encouraging in yourself a habit of spiteful talk; it will grow on you, if you are not careful about it. And those bad habits which we form are not destroyed in us when we get absolution on Saturday nights. The habitual drunkard who has just got absolved from the sin of his last drinking-bout is an habitual drunkard still.

That's one thing absolution doesn't remove, our bad habits. And there is another thing it doesn't remove, our debts. If you have taken something of value which doesn't belong to you, you are given absolution, but only on the condition that you will give back the thing you stole, or the money equivalent of it, if that is possible. But we must talk about restitution next Sunday. Meanwhile, there is another kind of debt which we incur by our sins; the debt of punishment which we owe, in this world or in Purgatory, in satisfaction for our sins. And absolution doesn't let us off that debt—otherwise there wouldn't be any Purgatory. What does help us to get rid of that debt is to get the indulgences which the Church offers; because every indulgence we get takes a bit off the amount that will be due from us to God's justice when we have been judged. But the sin itself, the black mark on our souls—that has gone; wiped out as clean as if it had never existed.

XXVI

The forgiveness of sins (2)

LAST SUNDAY I was talking about the theory of having
one's sins forgiven; now I want to talk about the practice of having one's sins forgiven, by which I mean
going to confession and getting sacramental absolution.
Remember, that is not the only way of getting
absolution. At any time you can make an act of
contrition, either by saying words over to yourself,
or by just telling God in your mind that you are sorry
for your sins and you won't, even if you get the
chance, sin again. It is advisable to make such an
act of contrition, if you are in a tight place; if you are
in a boat heading for a waterfall and don't seem to be
doing much good by trying to keep it away from the
waterfall, that is certainly the time to make an act of
contrition. Tell God that you love him, and that is
the reason why you are sorry for your sins, not
because of the waterfall, or because of hell. As for
the form of words, any form of words will do, however
short; " O my God, I'm sorry for my sins, and I will
never sin again " is quite enough. The important
thing is to fix your will in the right attitude about
your sins before you go over the waterfall. And if
it's a good act of contrition, what is called an act of
perfect contrition, God will forgive you your sins
and you will get to heaven in the long run whatever
your sins may have been. That's *one* thing to get

clear about; sacramental confession is not *absolutely* necessary. But of course if you *have* a priest in the boat, the best thing is to make him take your oar and confess your sins to him, especially if you have any fear that you may be in *mortal* sin.

However, you will want sometimes to go to sacramental confession. We've all got to go once a year, round about Easter; and there is one other occasion on which you have *got* to go to sacramental confession —when you are in mortal sin. If you say, " How *soon* do I go? " the simplest answer is, " Before you next go to Communion "; because, as we know, a Communion made when you are in mortal sin is a bad Communion, and a fresh sin, this time a sin of sacrilege. That's the simplest answer, but the best answer is, " As soon as possible ". Because there is always the chance of being run over by a lorry, and in any case no decent Christian wants to go about feeling that he is in mortal sin for a moment longer than he can help; it hurts.

Perhaps I ought to say a word or two about mortal and venial sin before we actually start preparing for confession. We all know what mortal sin is; you would say, " Mortal sin is when you cut yourself off from sanctifying grace ". But that would be wrong, because you should never begin a definition, especially when there are exams on, by saying " So-and-so *is when* ". You mustn't say, " A triangle *is when* a thing has three sides "; you must say, " A triangle is a three-sided figure ". So we will say, Mortal sin is sin which cuts us off from sanctifying grace. " Yes," you say, " I know that, but what I want to know is, How bad has it got to be? " Well, there are various things you can say about that. A sin can't be mortal if the material out of which it's made, so to speak, is something quite light. You can't commit a mortal sin by stealing another girl's rabbit-food, because rabbit-food isn't expensive enough; and you can't commit a mortal sin by making a face at a person, even if it's a very ugly face—though I suppose it might be a mortal sin of anger that made you make the face. You have to *know*, in order to commit a mortal sin, that the thing you are doing is wrong; it wouldn't be a mortal sin to put a clause in your will saying that you were to be cremated after death, if you didn't know that the Church disapproves of cremation. You have to *mean* what you are doing when you commit a mortal sin, to *think about* what you are doing. So you can't commit a mortal sin by not thinking about what you are doing in church; because you can't not think about what you are doing, if you are thinking about not thinking about what you are doing. Your action has to be a deliberate action; you can't commit a mortal sin by slapping somebody in the face quite automatically, without stopping to reflect whether it was a good thing to do—you just saw red and couldn't help it. And so on; there are lots of excuses that you can make; especially levity and curiosity, that is always coming in the moral theology books. But I'm not going to give you a long list of the excuses, for various reasons. One is, that we ought to try and avoid sin *even* if it's only venial, and therefore it's a bad thing to be always wondering how far it's safe to go in the way of sinning. And another reason is that it might help to give you what the moral theologians call " scruples ".

Do try to understand this clearly—that everything I'm going to say to you now, especially when I talk about mortal sins, is meant for your general information, and as a guide to your conduct later in life, when you will be in greater danger of committing mortal sins than you are at present. At present, the odds are enormously against any sin you confess on a Saturday evening being a mortal sin; and if you are doubtful whether it was, then you can be pretty certain that it wasn't. So don't for heaven's sake let's have anybody coming into the confessional and saying that she is afraid she MAY have committed a mortal sin by staying too long in the bath, because it will make me very angry indeed. Now let's get on to the practice of confession.

First there's preparation. I don't know at all how long you take over that here, because I don't hear you come into chapel at confession-time. Before Mass, when you all come in together, it sounds like a troop of cavalry; but on Saturday evenings you seem to slink in one by one. Anyhow, I suppose the nuns see that you don't come rushing into the box too suddenly. But, of course, we've got to think of when you go to confession in the holidays. How often *do* you go to confession in the holidays? Of course, I know a lot of you live a long way from a church, and it's hard to get about; but it's a bad habit to get into, not going to confession in the holidays, because it leads to the habit of not going to confession when you've left school. Try to go to confession sometimes in the holidays. Of course you would go if you were in mortal sin; but going to confession does give us grace to help in fighting against our *venial* sins, and every time we go it's worth going. Now let's get back to the practice of the confessional.

You want to get a clear idea of what your sins are before you go into the box. Not like the navvy who told the priest he'd broken all the commandments; and the priest said, " Surely not all? Have you committed a murder, for example? " And he said, " No, your Reverence, now you mention it, I don't think I have ". So the priest said, " You see, you haven't prepared yourself properly. You must go back to your place and come later on ". So the navvy went outside and said very loud to all the other navvies, " It's no good, boys; he's only hearing murders tonight ". Make up your mind clearly about whether you have murdered anybody, and if so how often. If you had, that would be a mortal sin, so you would be *bound* to mention that in your confession. If you forgot to mention it, honestly forgot, you would get absolution all right, but you would be bound to mention it *next* time you went to confession. Only because it's a *mortal* sin murdering people. If you forget a *venial* sin, there is no harm done and your absolution is perfectly all right, because we are not bound to mention venial sins in confession.

We are not bound to mention venial sins in confession, but they will do; they are sins, and so that gives us something to be absolved *for*. If you can't remember any sins at all, then mention some sin of your past life, saying, for example, " I've sinned against charity in my past life ", or, " I've sinned against the third commandment in my past life ", and that again gives you something to be absolved *for*. Because a sin, even when it is forgiven, is still something which *has happened*, and therefore we can still be sorry it happened; and as long as you are sorry about some sin of yours, you can go on being absolved. But I can't give you absolution if you don't mention any sin at all.

Having got your sins clear, and arranged them in some sort of order so that you are not likely to forget many of them, not the murders anyhow, what's the next thing? Listen carefully here, because it's a thing they don't tell you in books. *Before* you come into the confessional, make an act of contrition. You are always told in the books that you must make an act of contrition *while* the priest is actually giving you absolution. But some of us get muddle-headed when we try to do a thing on the spur of the moment like that, and we forget the words or get them mixed up, or we say them without meaning them because we are so flustered; and then we wonder afterwards whether it was a good confession. That's why I say, make an act of contrition *before* you leave the place where you are kneeling. *That counts*—even if you forget to make any act of contrition at all while you are in the box. Make another while you are being given absolution, by all means; it's the right thing to do. But make one *before* you go into the box, to be on the safe side, while you have still got all your wits about you.

Then you come into the box; and you start straight away, saying, " Bless me, Father, for I have sinned "; and then, as soon as the priest has said the blessing, or rather, at once, because he has probably got the blessing in first, go on and tell the priest your sins. Don't say the Confiteor in the box; that is another thing you ought to have done before you come in, only I forgot to mention it. Say the Confiteor *and*

make an act of contrition before you come into the
box, and when you are in the box just state your sins.
Don't be afraid of using colloquial phrases, or even
slang, the priest won't mind; but try to use words
that express their meaning clearly, and have only
one meaning. Don't say, for example, " I've been
nasty ", which might mean that you had been unkind
to somebody, or might mean that you had done something indecent. If there is anything that is specially
on your conscience, it is best on the whole to mention
that first, but of course that's not a rule, it's only a
piece of advice. Another thing, speak up. I don't
mean so much when you are going to confession here,
because I can just hear what you say, and the door
isn't very thick, and there are plenty of your friends
outside with their ears flapping. But when you are in
a proper confessional with a thick door, speak up,
because the priest may be a bit deaf. There was a
man at Oxford who used to eat glass, it was a kind of
parlour trick; and then his friends told him this was a
mortal sin, because it was practically suicide; so he
rushed off to the church and confessed to a very deaf
priest that he'd been eating glass, and the priest
thought he said " grass " and couldn't understand what
all the fuss was about. When you've finished, and the
priest has stopped talking to you in English, make your
act of contrition—your second act of contrition.
When the priest stops talking to you in Latin, and says,
" Go in peace and pray for me sometimes ", or words
to that effect, then (and not till then) go away; there's
nothing more, and you don't want to keep other people
waiting.

When you get back to your place, say your penance;

unless it's a very long penance and you've got to catch
a 'bus. You are not bound to say your penance at
any particular time; but if you find you haven't said
it by the next time you go to confession, you must
mention the fact to the priest. Having said your
penance, what's the next thing to do? Leave the
chapel? No, the next thing to do is to say a prayer
for the priest, as he asked you to. If you think that
priests hear confessions for fun, you are badly wrong;
say a prayer for the priest, who has probably got pins
and needles by this time. Then thank God for your
absolution. Then go away.

There's nothing more to do, unless reparation comes
into it. If you were to tell me you had stolen five
pounds' worth of linoleum, I should tell you to give
it back to the owner. If you'd lost the linoleum, I
should tell you to give back five pounds to the owner,
if and when you could raise the money. If you couldn't
remember for the life of you which shop it was you
took the linoleum from, I should tell you to give the
five pounds, if and when you could raise it, to the
Crusade of Rescue or the black babies. You are not
bound to give back the five pounds until you find
yourself with five pounds to give; but you are bound
to go on *meaning* to give back the five pounds. If you
stop *meaning* to give them back, that is a fresh sin of
theft, and you are back where you were. The only
other kind of reparation you may be told to make is,
if you've said something untrue which took away
somebody else's character, in a serious way. Not just
if you'd said, " So-and-so's a greedy pig ", but if
you'd said, " So-and-so cheated, and that's how she
got the prize for Scripture ". If that was untrue, I

might make you go and mention that it wasn't true
to the person you told the story to originally.

One other piece of advice I want to give you for
later life—at present, you get through your confessions
quickly enough. But don't, later on, get into the
habit of chatting to the priest in the confessional and
asking him if he knows where you can get a good
cook. Not because the priest has got pins and needles,
but because there are other people waiting. If you
want to chat to a priest, go round to the presbytery
door. The confessional is God's appointed means of
getting rid of your sins. What you want to do is to
state clearly what your sins are, and to make as good
an act of contrition as you can. Not necessarily an
act of *perfect* contrition; that is not necessary for
sacramental absolution, only when you are in the
boat going over the waterfall. Now, go away and
don't commit any sins, and come back on Saturday
and tell me about some sin you have committed in
your past life.

XXVII

I believe in the resurrection of the body,
and the life everlasting

I WAS TALKING to you last Sunday, if you remember, about sitting in the confessional on Saturday evenings, and how it's liable to give you pins and needles. And for fear you should think that that is a very heroic sacrifice on my part, let me recall to your memory the life of that very nice Saint, St. John Vianney, the Curé of Ars. I should have liked to give you a whole sermon about him, but I expect you know something about him already; if you want to know what he looked like, you've only got to go to the pigsties in the old stables, and you will find him there on a window-sill, because he is supposed to be rather good at looking after the health of farm animals. And if you think he would mind being in the pigsty, it shows you know very little about the Curé d'Ars. He used to spend about fourteen hours every day in the confessional. He came out for his lunch, which consisted of one or two potatoes, and he knew all his people and loved all his people and spent a lot of time visiting them, but, as I say, for fourteen hours every day he sat in the confessional, because penitents used to come to him from all over the world and queue up for absolution. He went to bed for three or four hours at night, but it didn't do him much good, because the devil, whom he used to call the *grappin* (which I think means the toasting-fork) used to come and pull him out of bed nearly every night, in the hope of persuading him to live differently. However, he went on living like that very happily till he was over seventy. And one day, talking to a friend, he said, " I know one old man who would look rather a fool if there were no future life ". Then he checked himself, and said, " Although, as a matter of fact, it is such an honour to serve God, that we ought to be proud and glad to do it, even if he gave us no reward at all at the end of it ".

Well, now we've got to the end of the *Credo* and we've got to think of our lives, and the reward we are going to get—perhaps. When God put man in an earthly paradise, and man made a mess of it, he could perfectly well have arranged, if you come to think of it, that Adam and Eve shouldn't have any children. And if they hadn't, one would be disposed to think, the situation would have been very neatly cleared up. Adam and Eve might have been allowed to spend a longish and fairly comfortable life, and then died, and been annihilated at death; or some kind of Limbo could have been invented, in which they could have lived on eternally as a pair of curiosities. But God, for some reason, didn't want to do that; he wanted mankind to be fruitful and multiply and fill the earth —and, when they died, to fill heaven. He was determined to have a lot of human beings about in heaven, sharing his happiness. That's curious, if you like. Of course, you may think it's jolly to live in a crowd; and perhaps you rather pity the poor nuns when the holidays come and they are left all alone by themselves. . . . Well, you know, Aldenham isn't too bad in the holidays. Anyhow, God wanted to have human beings about in heaven; and he left us with our free will, so that we could make use of the grace which he gives us and go to heaven if we did. If we didn't—that is the most mysterious thing of all, and a thing I suppose we shall never understand in this life, that God has left human beings free to go to hell, if they want to. He lets us have our way, like an indulgent Father, and if we insist on sending ourselves to hell, he allows us to do it.

There are plenty of difficulties about this last article in the *Credo*. We are talking about hell as well as heaven, when we say we believe in the resurrection of the body. Why it is that the lost souls in hell have to have their bodies restored to them after the general judgement is not immediately obvious. It isn't so that hell can hurt more; because the souls in hell do suffer, even before the general judgement, bodily pain. You see, all the pain which we feel in our bodies has got to get through to US, if it's to hurt. There's no harm in your *tooth* aching, if that were all. The trouble is that YOU have got a toothache. And these sensations of pain which we derive, on earth, through the body, are felt, now, by the souls in hell, although they have at present no bodies to feel them with; the process, somehow, is short-circuited. And the pains of hell go on for ever. The lost souls live in an eternal, changeless moment of despair. All that, as I say, is a thing which I don't suppose we shall ever understand in this life. There's a story of an Irishman who had doubts about hell, and the priest said to him, " Well, look at it this way, Pat; if there's no hell, where's Cromwell? " And he said, " Ah, your Reverence, I hadn't thought of that ". But somehow I don't know that even that makes it clear. All you can say is that if you're going to have a faith you have got to believe what it tells you, the uncomfortable parts as well as the comfortable ones.

However, it isn't necessary to be thinking about the uncomfortable parts *all* the time; and as we are getting to the end of the *Credo* and the end of the term let's try and finish up with a pleasant taste in our mouths. Let's pretend, you and I, that we are going to heaven. Mind you, I don't say that you are, still less that I am; but there's no harm in pretending. Even so, what are we going to make of this odd clause, " the resurrection of the body "? First, let's notice that for some reason the *Credo* we say is a mistranslation of the Latin. The *Credo* which is said by the universal Church hasn't got *Corporis Resurrectionem*, the resurrection of the body, as its last clause but one. Its last clause but one is *CARNIS Resurrectionem*, the Resurrection of the Flesh. And the flesh, in theological language (which comes from the Hebrew), means a great deal more than the body. It means the whole of your human nature, gifts of mind as well as of body, so long as they are natural, not supernatural, gifts. However, that takes us into complicated questions of theology; so let's just think about our *bodies* rising again, as they certainly will when the general judgement comes. Two common-sense questions naturally suggest themselves. One is, " How will it be possible for my body to rejoin my soul? Nothing will be left of my body by then, except a skeleton, if that ". Do you know a book of poems called *The Lays of the Scottish Cavaliers*?

Rather good, I think. In one of them Montrose, the Cavalier general who was killed by those very unpleasant people, the Covenanters, is made to say, " Go, nail my head to yonder tower, Give every town a limb; The God who made will gather them—I go from you to him ". That, in itself, seems rather a lot to hope for. But what about people who have been burnt in a fire; how are all their ashes going to be seccotined together again? And I think I'm right in saying that St. Thomas Aquinas, who always liked to allow for everything, discussed the question, What was going to happen about people who were eaten by cannibals? Because you might have a missionary saying, " Here, that's my big toe ", and a cannibal saying, " No, it's not, it's part of my stomach ".

Well, that isn't really as difficult a difficulty as it sounds. You see, it's a mistake to think of one's body as made up simply of so many bits of pink stuff. Your body is a living thing, which goes on changing all the time, as living things do. I think the scientific people tell us that every year every part of one's body is made up of different pieces of stuff compared with last year. I've still got a scar where I had an operation in the year 1906. The pieces of skin round that scar have changed thirty-seven times since then, but it's still there, which shows that I've still got the same body. The same body, though not made up of the same bits of skin; it isn't going to be difficult for us, then, to get back the *same* body in the next world, without going round looking for lost bits and pieces. If you come to think of it, your finger-nails aren't the same finger-nails, in a sense, as they were when the war started, because you've cut them a good many times since then—at least, I hope you have. But they are still *your finger-nails*. We shan't want to collect, when the general judgement comes, every single piece of stuff in the world that has once been our finger-nails; if we did, we should find ourselves in heaven with finger-nails about a mile long. No, God can give us back our bodies without bothering about all the pieces of skin and hair that once belonged to them.

And there's a third question that obviously suggests itself, about heaven. " What shall we want bodies *for?* " Think of the Saints in heaven now; our Lady's body, as we know, was taken up to heaven when she died, but that isn't true of St. Peter or St. Paul or any of the other Saints. Well, you can't imagine St. Peter, now, in heaven, complaining that he finds it rather uncomfortable not having a body. And therefore, if people can get on quite comfortably without their bodies till the general judgement, why can't they get on quite comfortably without their bodies after the general judgement? The answer to that, I think, is that body and soul were made for one another, and therefore both of them are in an unnatural state when you divide them, and demand to be reunited. It isn't that the soul is unhappy without the body; it can express itself otherwise, in heaven. But the body, which has been our companion all through our earthly pilgrimage, must not be permanently left out in the cold; that wouldn't be right. It, too, has its passport to eternity.

Not that, in heaven, our bodies will be in the same state as here. St. Paul tells us that our heavenly body won't be any more like our earthly body than the harvest which you cut in the summer is like the miserable little wizened seeds which you sowed in the late autumn. Our bodies, in heaven, will be ether-ealized; they will have none of the disabilities which they had on earth; there will be no getting pins and needles in heaven. Our bodies, here, are rather a nuisance in some ways, aren't they? Always running into things, or even into people. Our bodies in heaven, the theologians tell us, will offer no resistance to the touch, won't be solid. And another awkward thing about our bodies here is that they can't get about quick enough; we haven't quite finished drying them when somebody shouts " Last bell! " and we know that they ought to be in the refectory. That will be all right in heaven; we don't have the kind of body which takes time in moving from place to place. We shan't have bodily needs, either, which we have to satisfy, by eating and drinking, for example. Perhaps you don't regard that as very good news, but it's all right really. I'm sure, before now, you must have been late for meals because you were so excited about a game you were playing or a book you were reading? Well, if you like to put it that way, heaven means spending eternity in a state of such excitement that we shall be eternally late for our meals.

Some things the theologians tell us about heaven are just guess-work, and don't pretend to be more than guess-work. I think they say we shall all be thirty-three years of age, because that is the perfect time of life; I dare say it's true, but it's not in the *Credo*. They also tell us we shall all be good-looking; which is good news for some of us, and makes us wonder how our friends are going to recognize us; but that again isn't in the *Credo*. What I think you can say with perfect confidence, although as far as I know it isn't laid down officially anywhere, is that we shall know one another, and that part of our happiness in heaven will be due to finding ourselves reunited with those we love. We shall be united, too, with the Saints who prayed for us while we were on earth; we shall be united by a love we never dreamt of to our Lord himself.

And at the same time, when we get to heaven—if we get to heaven—we shall realize that the *Credo* was true, instead of just going on believing it was true. We shall be conscious of God as our Father; we shall recognize that everything which happened on earth was part of an almighty design. We shall find it quite natural that there should be three Persons in the Godhead, and that the second Person should be both God and man; God's only Son, our Lord, the visible object, now, of our worship, thanking us for all the little services we did for him. We shall have no difficulty in seeing that our Blessed Lady became his Mother and yet remained a Virgin. And although pain and suffering will then be only a distant memory of the past, no part any longer of our daily experience, we shall be able to look into and understand the sufferings which our Lord underwent when he was crucified by Pontius Pilate, all those billions and billions of years ago; we shall understand those sufferings, and take, from them, the measure of his love. We shall look down into the twilight world of Limbo, where once the patriarchs were; quite empty, now, only a record of the past; and the strange old people we used to see in stained-glass windows will be real people to us then; brought to light when our

Lord descended into hell. The Resurrection will not merely be something that seems quite natural; we shall be conscious of it at every instant as the very condition of our being; for we, too, shall have become part of that Risen Life which our Lord brought back with him from the tomb. We shall see him, ascended, sitting at the right hand of his Father, thank him for the merciful judgements he passed on us, living and dead. We shall feel the presence of the Holy Spirit within us; we shall know the Church for Christ's glorious Bride; we shall be in conscious communion with all the Saints; our sins, instead of looking black, will be rose-hued, like clouds at sunset, with the grace of final forgiveness. We shall be *risen*, soul and body; soul and body pulsing at every moment with the energies of an everlasting life.